# History Comes Home

# History Comes Home

*family stories across the curriculum*

**STEVEN ZEMELMAN**
**PATRICIA BEARDEN**
**YOLANDA SIMMONS**
**and PETE LEKI**

**STENHOUSE PUBLISHERS**
York, Maine

Stenhouse Publishers, P.O. Box 360, York, Maine 03909
www.stenhouse.com

Credit
Page 1: "(What a) Wonderful World" written by Sam Cooke, Herb Alpert, and Lou Adler. ©1959 Renewed 1987 ABKCO Music, Inc. All rights reserved. Reprinted by permission

Library of Congress Cataloging-in-Publication Data

History comes home : family stories across the curriculum / Steven
    Zemelman ... [et al.].
        p.    cm.
    Includes bibliographical references (p.    ).
    ISBN 1-57110-308-2 (acid-free paper)
    1. Genealogy—Study and teaching (Elementary)—United States.
I. Zemelman, Steven.
CS49.H57 1999
929'.1'071273—dc21                                        99-32842
                                                          CIP


Cover and interior design by Geri Davis, The Davis Group, Inc.
Cover quilt, Family Pictures, 1998, by Ellen Mitchell Elementary School,
Chicago Schools Quilts Millennium Project
Typeset by Technology 'N Typography

Manufactured in the United States of America on acid-free paper
05 04 03 02 01 00 99 9 8 7 6 5 4 3 2 1

# Contents

# Acknowledgments

*t*he creation of this book is a family history in itself, growing from intertwined roots. The Illinois Writing Project originally brought together Pat Bearden, Yolanda Simmons, and Steve Zemelman as they sought ways to deepen and strengthen writing in the classroom, and as they broadened their view to include reading and integrated curriculum. Our work in institutes and classrooms showed us that success in these school subjects depends on students' sense of themselves and how their lives connect (or fail to connect) with school. Pete Leki then joined us as the Center for City Schools at National-Louis University grew and we came to understand the centrality of families in the success of their children. Smokey Daniels and all the many talented and thoughtful Writing Project teacher leaders and workshop participants showed us the way as they shared their teaching experiences and deeply held beliefs about kids and education. Our Center for City Schools partner Marilyn Bizar passionately and humorously led us to think more clearly about teaching reading. Our dean, Linda Tafel, backed our efforts unceasingly as we spent more and more time in schools and writing books and grants. Pat, Yolanda, Steve, and Marilyn worked extensively with Mary Koerner of Roosevelt University, who showed us ways to help teachers examine multicultural issues in their classrooms.

Pat and Yolanda had the vision to begin creating strategies for learning about family history, at first in their own classrooms, and then in the rooms of Chicago teachers who welcomed and aided them, particularly Sharon West at Hurley School, Adrienne Brown-Murray at McDowell School, and Karen Malhiot and Eva Bynum at Jenner School. They were generously helped and encouraged in this work by Ted

Oppenheimer and the Oppenheimer Family Fund. Later, we met other teachers committed to family history—Suzanne Brion of Saline Middle School, Saline, Michigan, Jane Sanders Boyce at Hebron Middle School, Hebron, Indiana, Mary Tomasiak and Dan Jones at Tank Elementary in Green Bay, Wisconsin, and Tina Peano at the Best Practice High School in Chicago. Suzanne worked closely with Saline teammates Barbara Bureau, David Fiske, and Brian Lampman to make family history an interdisciplinary endeavor. We thank Deidre Searcy of Street-Level Youth Media for teaching us how to create two-minute videos. We know countless others have also created powerful classroom strategies that have filtered to us without our knowing or being able to thank them directly, just as beliefs and knowledge flow beneath the surface of our families for generations.

Then there are the students: intent faces, concentrating heads bent over paper, voices demanding attention to their stories, excitement and pride in the work, minds caught up in what they're discovering, oblivious to grades or tests or "standards." Theirs is the reality within which we must test all our supposedly good ideas. It's hard to say good-bye to the kids as they leave us at the end of the year, when we've learned so much from and about them.

And their families: willingly—or even hesitantly—answering repeated questions, sharing their knowledge of the past, proudly coming to family history fairs. Our book exists only to the extent that their history matters to them, and that they sense the value for the entire school community in generously offering their experience. Perhaps they also sense that such giving helps them reclaim the school as their own by providing them with a voice, instead of allowing the school to become a bureaucracy for the political benefit of others.

We've learned, too, what a debt we owe to our own families and their achievements and struggles. Pat spent a semester researching and gathering data on her own enslaved ancestors and her free heritage, the Parrishes, Hackworths, Frisons, Gates, and Walkers, who endured so she and her children could be here today. Each ancestral portrait Pat uncovered increased her euphoria and her sense of urgency to dig even deeper to reveal others, learn their stories, and in doing so, piece together the many parts that make her whole.

Yolanda cherishes childhood memories of coming home from school every day at noon to share a hot lunch with her mother, a homemaker, and her father, who owned a trucking company. He arranged his daily schedule to permit those lunches. Sitting around the kitchen table, they recounted the stories that had filled their mornings, stories that conveyed a powerful message Yolanda carried from the table: one's self-worth can be measured only by the value one acknowledges in others.

Pete's family immigrated to this country from Europe after the tragedies of World War II. His small immediate family was the only family he knew. Language, distance, and political barriers made meeting family back in the homeland difficult. But then, everyone's search is difficult, for different reasons. Pete's mother, Nina Leki, is both the swirling center of the family's story and its trilingual translator, filter, and interpreter. She is rare and enigmatic, an orchid in the woods.

Steve treasures his mother's stories of growing up within the Jewish community in St. Louis, and he thinks of all he's inherited from his father, who died when he was a teenager but who demonstrated, through founding and building a toy factory, what it meant to bring a productive new institution into the world. As a group, we marvel at how these pathways have wound through so many parts of the American experience, some full of light and others terribly shadowed, but ultimately bringing us together.

We thank our own families, spouses, and children, whose work and companionship give shape to our lives, just as our students imbibe meaning from those who nurture them. Our own valuing reminds us how crucial it is to connect school with our students' homes. Family history has been rich and energizing and enlightening for us. We hope it will be for you, too.

# Introduction

*Don't know much about history,*

*Don't know much biology.*

*t*he singer admits his ignorance of school subjects, and while he goes on to list the other major disciplines, history tops his list (and if we could, we'd substitute geography for biology since it's so crucial to our topic). What he *does* know about, and believes can create a wonderful world, is something far more personal: love. We can agree that he's got his priorities straight—what is ultimately more important in our lives than love and human relationships? Yet, as the song reminds us, too many people in this country experience the two worlds of school and relationships as if they are split by a wide gulf. And a great many students, if they feel forced to choose one over the other, will take you-know-which.

But does it really have to be that way? Wouldn't it be wise if we educators did more to reconnect these two worlds, the public/educational and the personal/social, so that they support and enrich each other instead of standing opposed? In fact, as we've observed in many effective classrooms, that's what really powerful teachers do again and again. In one way or another, they bring education home, and in the process, help students more readily engage with the first and more deeply understand the second. That's what this book is about: linking family and individual histories with the public history taught in school, to make a big chunk of the curriculum—social studies, history, writing, and literature—more meaningful for children.

One thing we do know, through the family history investigations at Jenner School in Chicago's Cabrini-Green housing projects: the singer of those famous lyrics, Sam Cooke, is the great uncle of student Jasmine Hines. Family history study is like that—"only six degrees of separation," as people like to say. Although not every student has a famous relative, it's surprising how many do, and surprising how many more relatives and ancestors have witnessed or participated in important historical events.

When principal Lucille White agreed to pilot the Family History Project at McDowell Elementary School on Chicago's South Side, little did the fifth graders dream of the discoveries they were about to make. In the course of preparing and giving oral reports on their research findings and comparing their kinship charts, the students discovered they had quite a bit in common. Shaun, Nick, Akeen, and Eric are cousins. Andrea, Andura, Gread, Tyra, Christian, Darius, Robert, Chris, Julie, Tenisha, Veronica, and Jade have some of the same surnames, places, and dates on their kinship charts.

Seven students have famous relatives:

- Oprah Winfrey is Christina's cousin.
- Former U.S. Senator Carol Moseley-Braun is Andura's and Andrea's cousin.
- Lorraine Hansberry is Kerri's aunt.
- Langston Hughes is James's cousin.
- Sachel Paige is Danielle's cousin.
- Gread McKinnis I (Negro baseball league) is Gread's grandfather.
- Suzanne Douglas (*Parenthood* star) is Jenea's cousin.

When Pat Bearden arrived in the classroom for her regular visit shortly after these discoveries were made, students crowded around to relate the exciting news. After calming everyone down, Pat posed the researcher's question: "How can you prove this? How can you back up your claim?" The students went to work. Kerri brought in a family copy of Lorraine Hansberry's birth certificate and her own little book of poems that she had written. Danielle found background information about her cousin Sachel Paige, and Gread McKinnis found data about his grandfather Gread I, in a book on the Negro baseball leagues.

Christina Winfrey, eleven, always knew there was something unique about her name. After tracing her family roots back to her great-great-grandfather as shown in Figure I.1, she discovered that her second cousin twice removed is television talk show personality Oprah Winfrey. "I was so excited when I found out," said Christina with a big smile. "I found out from my grandfather that she had come to last year's family picnic in Mississippi. I'm trying to get her to come out to the school." She has corresponded with Oprah about her discovery, as shown in Figure 4.8.

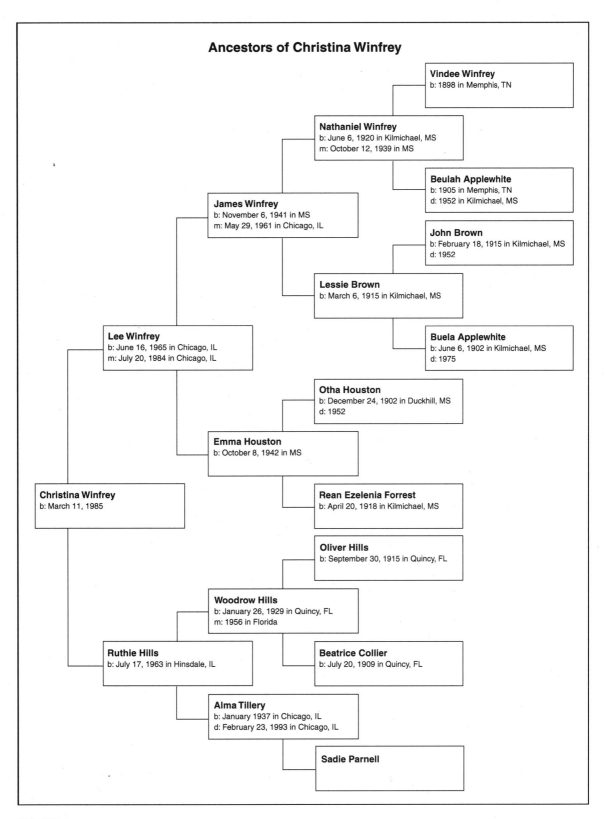

FIGURE I.1

Ancestor chart for Christina Winfrey. Vindee Winfrey was Oprah Winfrey's grandfather's brother.

What about students who do not have famous relatives? "We all have relatives, extended family members, and ancestors that we can look up to. We all have heroes and she-roes in our families who we can admire. We just have to take the time to find out who they are," student Courtney Reed responded. "My ancestors were a part of history. That makes them famous to me."

"Just because our people's names are not in books, it doesn't mean we're not famous," Veronica interrupted. "My people still helped to make America great. And just by living, we are part of history."

"I didn't really like history at first, but I really like it now," said Gread McKinnis, who, like other students, can now trace family members and discuss the major historical events that have taken place during his lifetime. "I've lived through the Million Man March, the O. J. trial, three Bulls championships, and the Oklahoma bombing. It's something that I'll be able to tell my kids about."

It's not like this everywhere. In far too many classrooms, kids are marched through history textbooks, lectures, and quizzes with little to show for it. Studies have repeatedly shown that American students are not strong on historical knowledge, nor do they regard history as a particularly exciting subject. In 1994, the National Assessment of Educational Progress (NAEP) administered a test to assess the historical knowledge of 22,500 public and private school students across the country. The study produced some discouraging findings:

- Nearly six in ten high school seniors lacked a basic understanding of the subject.
- Only 40 percent of fourth graders knew why the Pilgrims came to America.
- Only 41 percent of high school seniors could define the Monroe Doctrine.
- Only 30 percent of high school seniors could identify the chief goal of American foreign policy after World War II.
- 73 percent of high school seniors did not know that the Camp David accords promoted peace between Egypt and Israel.

—ALEXANDRA S. BEATTY ET AL.,
*NAEP 1994 U.S. History Report Card*

But it's not entirely the kids' or the teachers' fault, for in many ways we are an ahistorical country. Many immigrants who arrived over the decades and centuries wished to forget, or were forced to abandon, the histories and cultures they left behind. Adults move away from families, and families move repeatedly to new neighborhoods or cities in search of a better life, leaving old connections behind. And as any politician can tell you when he looks ahead to an election several years in the future, our country thrives on political and historical amnesia. So making the subject of history meaningful in any school setting is a continuous challenge.

Children in poor and economically disadvantaged areas face additional obstacles. The language and middle-class culture of school can seem foreign to them, implying that somehow their families and backgrounds are lesser, that school has nothing to do with who they are. If your future seems starkly circumscribed, studying other times or places may seem painful, a reminder of how trapped you feel in the place you live now. The existence of great heroes and leaders from various minority groups are distant abstractions, adding irony to the situation. But what if those heroes weren't so far off after all? What if they turned out to be your own aunts, uncles, or cousins?

It is this need for connection, for inner-city students, that started us on this project. One November day in 1991, Pat Bearden asked Calvin, a fifth grader who had come by her third-grade room after school, where he was going for Thanksgiving. "Down South," he replied.

PAT: Where down South?
CALVIN: I don't know.

Understandable enough. Kids hear people use such phrases. But Pat asked him to find out, inquired after the holiday, and was troubled by his continued disengagement.

CALVIN: I forgot.
PAT: Why don't you ask your mother to tell you?
CALVIN: She didn't go with us, and my dad doesn't live with me.

Pat had to search her soul. If he'd reached fifth grade and didn't seem to care where his family came from, lacked the pride or curiosity, shouldn't school attempt to provide this missing link in his experience? Without it, how could teachers ever make history and geography—his history and geography, all of our history and geography—meaningful and exciting for him?

It is crucial that school curriculum for all students reconnect history with their own lives and that it value their backgrounds and their places in the American community. The aim is not to Balkanize and separate this country's cultural groups, but by valuing them, to link them with a larger whole. According to Emily Style, a Madison, New Jersey,

English teacher and diversity coordinator, students must be provided with both windows and mirrors—windows that show them views of others, views of the larger world, and the knowledge they will need to flourish within it, and mirrors that help them learn about and value themselves and their individual cultures.

These two kinds of knowledge, windows and mirrors, can enrich and support each other. When teachers allow students to use knowledge about their families to support the learning of new knowledge about the larger world, they send students a powerful message: your family members and members of your ethnic group played significant roles in shaping our country—significant enough to spend sustained time studying them. This connection not only creates a sense of inclusion, but establishes emotional ties to the topic, without which true learning rarely occurs.

Family history offers a way out of the divisive trap of racializing our identities. The ominous divides of race are bridged by the actual complexity of our collective past, and by the great lesson our histories deliver: *in many ways, we are all similar.* Our families and peoples the world over have worked, struggled, fought through wars and hard times, adjusted to technology, and made it to this place and day. Further, by focusing on ethnic origins, migrations, and pathways, identity is constantly enriched and expanded. All of us come from somewhere. Family trees branch into a glorious, bushy complexity, rich with a million stories. And our stories are linked.

The family history project offers a way into the *home* as a source of knowledge, experience, and expertise. This is not "prying" into private family concerns. Rather, the dialogue between child and family gives children practice in innumerable academic skills, and simultaneously honors and strengthens the family and community. The family history project is like Campbell's vegetable soup—"It's all in there."

The curriculum described in this book came to life in everyday classrooms in some of the most neglected urban neighborhoods, as experienced teachers sought to fulfill the polar needs that students have for windows and mirrors, public knowledge and personal connection. It worked for us, and it can work for you. Pat Bearden and Yolanda Simmons created the Getting to Know You Culturally exercise that begins the family history project, because they needed a culturally sensitive community-building exercise. They found that using pair interviews for students to share background about their name and their family's place of origin was a lively and effective way to do this. But then we realized we could use this information for other social studies learning. When Pat received a Golden Apple award (given to outstanding teachers in the Chicago metropolitan area each year), she used the semester-off scholarship to travel south and investigate her own family history. She immediately recognized its potential for her students. Through a series of grants from the Oppenheimer Family Fund, she and Yolanda developed the rest of the activities in this book for their own classrooms and in other Chicago schools.

We watched as students skipped lunch and hung around after school to learn about their own histories and to complete displays relating personal histories to public history. Parents and grandparents, stepparents, foster parents and guardians, community members, local business people, and representatives of cultural institutions became eager teaching partners.

Meanwhile, all of us, working with the Illinois Writing Project and National-Louis University's Center for City Schools, observed repeatedly how students' reading and writing bloomed when we connected classroom subjects with the kids' cultural backgrounds. As a parent involvement leader with the center, Pete Leki began using the same activities in his parent workshops. It wasn't long before children and parents were working together to put on family history fairs in inner-city schools around Chicago, and we provide examples of this in many chapters of the book.

However, it's essential for a successful family history project that teaching not just cover the *content* described in this book, but mirror the inclusiveness and engagement of that content in the *classroom strategies* we use to teach it. Otherwise, it's all too easy to march students through one more teacher-designed and -led curriculum unit that implicitly tells them they really aren't that important in their school room after all. We've therefore structured the family history activities around the key strategies that national standards documents have characterized as best practice learning. These documents tell us that learning in all subjects must become more student-centered and experiential, more authentic, collaborative, and challenging. We've also included guidance in how to use many of the strategies that enact these principles in the classroom. As Harvey Daniels and Marilyn Bizar describe in their book *Methods that Matter*, these are:

- ◆ integrated, negotiated learning—connecting subject areas and including students in decisions about the topics to be studied;
- ◆ small-group activities—students working collaboratively, not just to prepare for tests, but to gather, analyze, and share information;
- ◆ representing to learn—including formal and informal writing and the arts;
- ◆ classroom workshop—structured time in which students

work on individually chosen projects while the teacher holds conferences with individual students or small groups;

♦ authentic experiences—moving the classroom out into the world, bringing the world into the classroom, and focusing on large topics with meaning and significance in students' lives;

♦ reflective assessment—helping students set their own goals, helping them reflect on their own learning, and linking assessment meaningfully with instruction.

If you've hesitated to try student-negotiated curriculum planning, or writing workshop, or portfolio assessment because you fear it will distract from covering curriculum, you'll find in this book a collection of easy steps for putting these to work as your students are learning valuable subject matter.

Of course, when instruction is more student-centered, as with family history, there is no single textbook to follow. Instead, the stories of the students' lives—their family and community histories—create the context and the content for learning. This student-centered curriculum becomes a common body of cultural knowledge, loaded with ethnic and historic background that can be used as a base for learning across the curriculum. Some teachers worry that such student-centered learning has no "structure," no clear direction. But the activities and the information students gather ensure that the family history project has strong bones and plenty of meat on them as well.

Still, what about the mandated curriculum in our districts, all the content in social studies and English we're required to teach nowadays? How can we fit in this additional topic? The answer is that integrated study projects such as family history invariably cover much of the required curriculum, but do it in a more natural order than the march of fragmented content items usually listed in state or district standards guides. To show how you can reassure yourself that necessary content is covered, we provide an example in Chapter 8 explaining how one group of middle school teachers easily "back-mapped," comparing topics covered in a family history project with the official district curriculum list of required social studies topics and concepts. Teachers usually are surprised that far more of the curriculum gets covered through the project than they expected. Specific topics that are missed can be taught separately as needed. Thus a teacher can creatively guide his or her students down self-generated roads of inquiry, roads that link the students to the subject matter through meaningful personal connections, while they simultaneously fulfill the official curriculum requirements.

This book is organized to make it easy to use. Some teachers new to our approach may wish to try one or two activities first to get their feet wet. But if you go step by step, the workshops will move students through a sequence of deepening engagement and understanding of family history and its links with formal social studies content, in the following order:

**Framing the Topic:**    A brief introduction to set the stage for the project and involve students in as much planning and direction as possible (we recognize that we've set the overall topic, rather than having students pose their own initial questions in a fully negotiated approach—though family history does involve many of the themes students invariably bring up: identity, race and ethnicity, war and peace).

**Getting to Know You Culturally:**    An interview activity that allows students to access prior knowledge of their cultural backgrounds, discover questions and gaps in their knowledge, and build community and interest in one another's history.

**Family Interview and Creating a Classroom Profile:**    Preparing students for, and guiding them through, the gathering of information on their family's history, customs, and beliefs. Then students compare and chart the information to gain a sense of common and differing family experiences.

**Writing and Other Forms of Expression in Family History:**    A variety of strategies and topics for documenting and sharing the powerful information students assemble as they pursue their family history investigations.

**Creating a Kinship Chart:**    Helping students deepen their knowledge of family ancestors and origins by charting a family tree and gathering further information from census data and other sources.

**Family History and Formal History Time Lines:**    Understanding historical development by placing important family events on a time line and comparing it with national and world history time lines.

**Two-Minute Videos:**    Using visual representation for students to share the experiences, ideas, and values they've uncovered in their study of family history.

**Meaningful Assessment of Family History Study:**   Ways to evaluate student work on the family history project so that students are encouraged and challenged to improve, and so that good instruction and meaningful learning is supported rather than undermined.

Each workshop (chapter) is organized as follows:

- ◆    An introduction to and explanation of the specific workshop.
- ◆    A how-to guide to the activity.
- ◆    A list of learning objectives your class can accomplish through the workshop.
- ◆    Case studies and student samples (we call these Reality Checks) to illustrate how the workshops happen in real classrooms and the results you can expect, from primary grades to adult learners.

Family history study is a good medicine, giving reflective time an honored place in the school curriculum. In the great hurried rush of our lives and our teaching, the family history project permits us to stop, linger, listen, and help our students gather a treasure chest of knowledge. And we pursue this treasure through community endeavor. In our search for meaning and wisdom, it is our communities and families that sustain us, that lift us up when we need help, allowing us to reach high. Learning about them can honor our similarities and differences as great gifts, and allow us to carry on.

That is the model we carry into our work in the schools, as described in this book. Executed with love and care, these workshops will help build your school community, show students the great mysterious path that brought us here, and guide them to envision a place up the road worth struggling for.

## We believe

When students are given opportunities to identify how their families
fit into public history, they are more easily able to:
Make sense of the past
Understand why knowledge about the past helps give
meaning to the present
Envision themselves in the context of world and national citizenry.

## We believe

Integrating family history into the social studies curriculum:
Makes learning what it should be—engaging, inclusive, and purposeful
Encourages students to imaginatively process historical information
Promotes critical thinking and inquiry-based learning,
Which results in deeper understandings of historical
concepts and content
Expands and deepens students' prior cultural knowledge
And enriches the schema students draw upon
to understand their world.

—STEVEN ZEMELMAN, PATRICIA BEARDEN,
YOLANDA SIMMONS, AND PETE LEKI

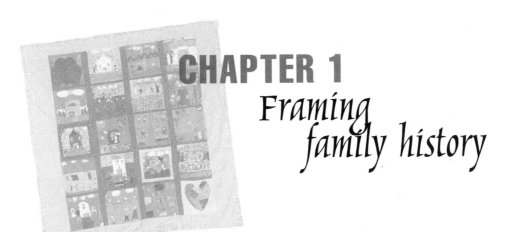

# CHAPTER 1
## *Framing family history*

You've just been introduced to a new acquaintance and immediately take note of the person's clothes, facial expression, and extent of eye contact. You ask a question and sense whether the response is forthcoming, shy, or guarded. You notice whether the person seems interested in you. This moment may not entirely determine the course of the friendship, but it certainly sets the initial direction. How you introduce the family history project to your students is equally important. When we teachers are enthusiastic about a topic, it's tempting to just dive right in and put kids to work. But it's crucial to lay some groundwork first.

The more you involve students in the goal setting and planning of the project, the more ownership and commitment you'll see throughout its execution. We aren't presenting this program as a fully student-directed or negotiated project, though we'd be pleased to see it approached that way, as more teachers learn to help students make choices in their studies. However, even within the broad outlines of the teacher's expectations, students can consider and suggest many options from the very start:

♦ Goals and objectives—what are students hoping to learn?
♦ Possible activities—visit several ethnically focused museums? Bring in some grandparents to talk to us? Hold a family history fair for the rest of the school?
♦ Which of our relatives might we interview?
♦ How shall we present information—posters, a class book, short videos, Web pages?

You, the teacher, will learn much from this about students' expectations and prior knowledge. The students will gain a sense of where the project is heading, so they can fit the initial pieces of what they're learning into a larger context. And they'll see that you consider the topic important and are committed to seeing the project through.

Of course, an introduction cannot on its own alter students' views and understandings. That level of learning and change requires the full cycle of the family history project. But it is important to begin the process so that from the very start, students' needs and motivations are addressed and respected. The key activities in this introduction are the teacher's sharing of a piece of his or her own family history, some small- and large-group discussion to start children planning together and telling what they know about their own background, and listing some of their goals and expectations for the project.

## how-to guide
### STEP 1:
### SETTING THE STAGE WITH BACKGROUND ON FAMILY STRUCTURES

The teacher introduces this first workshop by describing and helping students discuss various types of family structures. Present some statistics on family structures in the 1990s. Kids are less likely to feel alone or ostracized if they know, for example, that:

- 31.7 percent of U.S. family households with children under eighteen were headed by a single parent in 1998;
- 6 percent of families with children under eighteen were composed of extended family members instead of parents;
- 58.8 percent of mothers with preschool children were employed in 1998;
- there are 165 divorced people for every 1,000 married people in the United States. But 75 percent of divorced women remarry; therefore many children have a stepparent.

—Sources: U.S. Bureau of the Census, *Household and Family Characteristics,* (Current Population Reports #P20–515, March 1998); U.S. Bureau of the Census, *Marital Status and Living Arrangements* (Current Population Reports #P20–514, March 1998); Bureau of Labor Statistics, *Employment Characteristics of Families, 1997*; The Divorce Centers, Inc., *Parents Handbook.*

Share this information to help students feel comfortable about themselves and their family structures. What are some of the various ways that family members connect so that individuals can help each other?

- Large extended families versus small nuclear units.
- Visits back and forth among relatives living in various cities, regions, or other countries.
- Children living periodically with one parent and then the other, or for periods with a grandparent.
- Multiple family members running a store or business together.

Mention several of these arrangements, and ask students to describe ways that their own families work. Emphasize our common bonds. *We all have family. We all come from somewhere. We all have stories.*

## STEP 2:
## STUDENTS LIST REASONS WHY FAMILY HISTORY IS IMPORTANT

Now invite students to list reasons why family history could be important, record these on a sheet of butcher paper, and post it on the wall. If students are hesitant, ask them to write lists working in twos or threes, and then have reporters share reasons from their lists. Some common reasons students may give (depending on their age):

- You can find out where your family came from.
- You can find out if you have any famous ancestors.
- You can learn what life was like for your parents and grandparents when they were kids.
- You can see if some of your ancestors looked like you or acted like you.
- You can discover whether people in your family did any special kinds of things like fight in the Civil War, or hunt bears, or travel to distant places.
- You can learn whether some of your ancestors are from different cultural groups, such as Native American, or Irish, or Egyptian, even if your family doesn't consider itself a part of that group.

## STEP 3:
## THE TEACHER SHARES HIS OR HER FAMILY HISTORY

Modeling is always helpful, and students are unceasingly fascinated with the facts and shapes of their teachers' lives (which itself tells us something about students' hunger to find more meaningful links with school). Take some time to talk about your own family's origins, traditions, and migration patterns, to spark kids' interest and illustrate the kinds of things they will learn during the project. You may need to do some telephoning and research to fill in a few blanks, in which case you'll discover some of the excitement and insight that your students will soon be experiencing.

Steve tells about his grandfather:

When I interviewed my mother to learn about my family's past, I uncovered some surprising facts. My mother's father arrived in the United States at the age of eleven or twelve in the 1870s, with two brothers and an older cousin, all determined to escape the draft in Russian-controlled Lithuania. Young Jewish men were treated very brutally in the military there, and they feared they might be killed if they didn't leave. On first arriving, my grandfather, Benjamin Mayer, worked in New York making picture frames, finally settling in St. Louis to be close to other relatives. He and a few other family members briefly moved to Oklahoma when that territory was opened for settlement in the land rush of 1893, claiming a piece of land that now sits in downtown Oklahoma City. However, after suffering from loneliness and a lack of the kosher food that was important to them, they soon gave up their homestead and returned to St. Louis, unable to foresee that the land would someday be extremely valuable.

Dad Mayer, as people often called him, always loved children and enjoyed playing with them, just as I and my own sons do now. For a while Dad Mayer owned a grocery store, but he was never a good businessman, and during the depression couldn't resist providing groceries on credit for neighbors who were unable to repay him. As a result, the grocery store failed. In this, too, I see echoes, both positive and negative, in my own behavior and that of my children. My mother had hoped to go to college and become a teacher, but the family's hard times prevented her from ever doing this. I did not learn of this until after I had begun my own teaching career.

## STEP 4:
## STUDENTS BEGIN TO TELL WHAT THEY KNOW ABOUT THEIR FAMILIES

Once you've shared some of your own discoveries, ask your students questions that invite them to share some of their family stories, as well as to acknowledge the many blanks that will need to be filled in:

- What are some traditions celebrated in your family's culture?
- Are there special customs your family follows?
- Have you ever wondered why you do some of the things you do, eat what you eat, feel like you do?
- When did your people migrate to this city? Why did they leave the place where they had lived?
- Does your family have reunions? Why do people do this?
- If you don't know much about your family's background, what do you think are some things you might try to learn about?
- What part do you think your family has played in our city's history? In U.S. history? Every family contributes to our being here in various ways. What might your family's contribution be?
- Are there children in the class who have no access to their family origins and may need the option of inquiring about the history of their broader national or ethnic background?

Again, if your students are hesitant to answer or shy about speaking up, ask them to talk in pairs first, one question at a time, and go around the room getting responses.

## STEP 5:
## SETTING GOALS AND EXPECTATIONS FOR THE PROJECT

Finally, explain to the students your purpose for this unit of study: *to learn more about our families and cultures, and then to place ourselves and our families within the history of the community, the country, and the world.* Ask students to list the things they expect to learn about themselves. What kinds of information should they look for? How might they present it to the class or the rest of the school? How might the students change their ideas about themselves and their family as a result of studying family history? Record the students' suggestions and expectations on butcher paper and display the lists in the room. This provides a set of ideas, goals, and expectations that can be used to execute the project. They can be reviewed later, to help students see what they've learned and to realize their surprise that there is much more to this subject than they originally realized.

## goals and objectives

By the end of this session, your class will have accomplished the following:

- Begun to develop an attitude of openness and appreciation for the various lifestyles, family types, and ethnic and cultural experiences that fellow students bring with them.
- Established an initial set of questions and expectations about the learning that will take place in the family history project.
- Participated in planning, by contributing ideas for the direction and execution of the project.
- Demonstrated a baseline for observing growth in student knowledge and understanding about their own and others' family histories.
- Demonstrated a baseline for observing student understanding of the significance of local and national history in their lives.

## what we got—reality checks
### EXPECTATIONS IN MRS. MCCANN'S THIRD GRADE, HURLEY SCHOOL

When we asked third-grade students what they looked forward to learning by studying family history, they realized the possibilities for satisfying their curiosities about the past. They responded eagerly as follows:

ERIC: I want to know where my parents met.

ROBERTO: How did they live?

ADRIANNA: When did my parents get married?

KURT: I want to find out when my grandparents came to Chicago.

ERICA: I want to know how my ancestors traveled here. My mom was born in Mexico, but she was a little girl when she came here. So does she still remember things about Mexico?

AMANDA: I want to find out what my ancestors ate. There were different kinds of food.

> WILLIE: Where did my mom and dad go to school? Was school
>     different than now?
>
> VICTOR: What did my mom and dad do when they were kids?

Of the class of twenty-five, twelve didn't know where their forebears came from. Twenty-one wondered how their parents met. Everyone wanted to know what school was like for their parents. When the subject of holidays came up, about half didn't know about the Mexican tradition of Day of the Dead, reflecting the ethnic split in the class which was about half Mexican American. Everyone looked forward to hearing about families and groups that were different from their own.

## WHEN PARENTS AREN'T IN THE PICTURE: MARTIN LUTHER KING HIGH SCHOOL, 1992

Occasionally, students will be resistant at the start of the family history project because the topic brings up strong feelings, or because they cannot possibly obtain information about their original family. Some children may be adopted or living in foster homes or institutional settings, and have limited access to information about their family origins. The teacher must use his or her best judgment about when privacy must be respected, when an assignment needs to be broadened, when a substitute activity must be made available, or when it is important to encourage a student onward. Throughout this curriculum, teachers must keep in mind that its goals are to help students develop pride and knowledge about their backgrounds, make meaningful connections with the school curriculum, and learn to respect one another, rather than just complete a particular assignment.

Yolanda Simmons learned this lesson early on in a vivid moment with James, a tenth grader. As the students in Yolanda's class at King High School started brainstorming ideas about why they should study family history, James suddenly bolted from his seat.

> JAMES: Just go on and send me to the dean's office.
>
> MRS. SIMMONS: Why would I do that, James?
>
> JAMES: 'Cause I ain't gonna talk about my father. I ain't gonna
>     write about him either, and I sure ain't gonna do no research
>     on him!
>
> PATRICE: What you complaining about, James? My dad won't call
>     me until I'm eighteen. Says he can't be stuck with child
>     payments. After I'm eighteen, he says we can talk.
>
> LATASHA: Never met my dad. What you running from? We're

getting older now. Time to face the facts, to deal with ourselves.

BETTIE: Run all you want, James. Just gonna end up running into yourself.

James slammed the door behind him and strode off down the hall. The next day, as James entered the room, we all took a deep breath and held it.

JAMES: Okay if I pass out the family history portfolios, Mrs. Simmons?

Relieved, we smiled. Our smiles told James we understood his feelings and would be there to support him. We were on our way to becoming a real community of learners, willing to take risks, explore ourselves, our families, and our histories.

## WORKING WITH PARENTS

When parents are available to participate in family history activities not just at home but in their own workshops, it provides a tremendous boost for the kids' efforts. Parents can add information and perspective, as well as model the kinds of investigation we are asking the students to undertake. And in locations where poverty has bred discouragement, the activities build pride for the adults as well as the children. Adopted and foster children can be linked with the larger community and its heritage(s). In fact, in Chapters 5 and 6, we've provided examples of a parent who was raised in an orphanage and was gratified to find legal records about her own parents.

Pete Leki remembers the first time he broached family history with a group of parents at Jenner Academy, in the Cabrini-Green public housing complex of Chicago, and discovered that just as with children, he needed to help participants deal with the uncertainty surrounding the material they were delving into. He invited Pat Bearden in to talk about her family history and to show pictures of her great-grandmother Fredonia and others in her family's past. She announced that her ethnic roots are African, Native American, and Irish. The room was perfectly still as pictures of ancestors were passed around, some light skinned, some dark, some in between.

One woman spoke up. "Aren't you afraid? Afraid of what you might find out?"

Pat said, "Yes, I *was* afraid. No, I'm not afraid now. We've all got skeletons in the closet. We all have things in our past that we would rather not have happened. But here we are! This is a celebration. Wherever we came from and whatever we've been through, it's just who we are. And here we are today, and the more we look back, the more we can say, 'Wasn't that something!'"

Pat went on to tell the story about her grandfather who went to prison, convicted of murder for being part of the Atlanta race riots in 1906. As the story was told by Grandpa Alex Walker, a county officer was shot and killed during the riots. Alex was arrested, charged, and sentenced to life imprisonment. With the help of his Irish grandfather, Wright Read, who was a policeman, Alex was released from prison after serving just four years of the sentence. On the night of his release, Alex moved his family to Birmingham, Alabama, where he worked as a porter in a barbershop, and then at the Bessemer Steel works. Pat was able to corroborate this story by finding an article in the *Atlanta Constitution* newspaper. "Is this history or what?" she asked. "Aren't we part of the history of this country?"

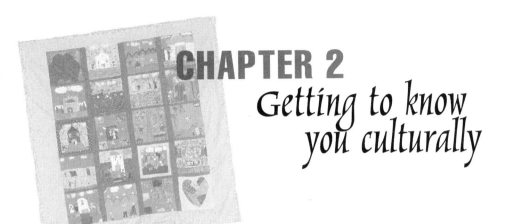

# CHAPTER 2
## Getting to know you culturally

*i*t's surprising how little students know about one another, even though they may sit side by side for months or years. We also find, in staff development workshops with teachers, that they, too, lack knowledge of their colleagues' histories and interests—perhaps because schools aren't really organized to support much interchange among their staff. We're still living with the nineteenth-century large-factory model for running schools, even though the rest of the world has entered an age of constant computer chat and e-mail.

Getting to Know You Culturally is a pair-share, in-class interviewing workshop that helps students become acquainted with one another's background, so that they begin to see each other as resources for cultural knowledge and understanding. The information is gathered by one student from another as they work in pairs informally with a short list of questions. This is one of the *primary* activities of the family history project, the foundation for an emergent, student-centered curriculum, for it not only begins the process of gathering and sharing information, but helps to build a strong and trusting classroom community.

It's essential to take time with activities such as this one and allow them to create an accepting tone in the classroom. Your students will not discuss their family structures or histories if they do not feel at ease with you and their peers. They will hesitate to examine and connect the stuff of their lives to the school curriculum if you do not share information about yourself. They need assurance that they can trust you and the class with the information and that it is being shared to deepen learning, not simply to pry into people's privacy. It is up to the teacher to build this trust so students can function as a community of learners. And so we've designed many of the activities in the family history project to serve double duty—to further content learning and to develop the class as a group at the same time.

Time taken for this activity is well spent. Students get initial practice in interviewing someone—in this case, a classmate their own age, which is a comfortable way to start. They must take notes and check their accuracy. They get practice in giving short oral presentations and writing explanatory essays. They gain fresh knowledge about classmates, which helps to build links and relationships among them. Each student sees that he or she has information to contribute that adds to the whole. And most discover questions they don't yet have answers for, about themselves and their families.

## how-to guide
### STEP 1:
### ORGANIZE PAIR INTERVIEWS

Pair up your students. If you have an ethnically diverse classroom, it's a good idea to pair children from different backgrounds. In general, it helps to match students who do not already know each other well, so they can learn something new about their partners right away. Each student will ask his or her partner the questions below and record the answers on index cards that you provide. (As a variation, similar questions can be generated by the students themselves in the whole group, or can be modified to bring out particular kinds of information needed in the curriculum.) Aim for an atmosphere of fun and informality. The noise level will quickly rise and peak as students warm to the task, laugh, and relax with each other. This is good.

### Questions for the Interview

- What is your full name?
- Whom are you named for?
- What does your name mean?
- What is your favorite childhood memory?
- Where were you born? If you weren't born locally, when did you or your family come to this city?
- If you lived in other places before settling here, where did you live?
- Where were your parents and grandparents born?
- Where do your ancestors originate from within the United States? Outside the United States?

- ◆ Do you attend family reunions?
- ◆ Has anyone in your family ever recorded your family history?

## STEP 2:
## PREPARATION FOR INTRODUCING PARTNERS TO THE CLASS

After the partners have interviewed each other, give them time to look over the information they have gathered, and explain that they'll be introducing their partners to the rest of the class. Demonstrate for them how an introduction might go:

*"Hello. My name is Michael, and I would like to present to you Tabitha Reilly . . ."*

*"I interviewed a very special person today. His name was Tadeus Skopek . . ."*

After students have reviewed their notes, have them run through the introduction with their partners to make sure it is accurate and that they correctly pronounce the name. While students are preparing, here's a touch you can add that will heighten their interest and sense that this project is truly about *them*: Go around the room with a camera and take a picture of each child. If the kids are old enough, pass the camera around and have them take photos of each other. These pictures will be added to written portraits of the children composed by their partners.

Finally, to prepare the group to give and receive the introductions attentively, ask the children what they think a good introduction sounds like. What should they be listening for? Ask them what it feels like to speak in front of a group. What are the responsibilities of the audience? What does it mean to be a good and supportive listener? Jot some of the key responses onto a flip chart or chalkboard so they're available as reminders if needed. Because school emphasizes communication with the teacher, students aren't always accustomed to really listening to one another. You can ask that two or three students give responses or ask questions after each introduction, to create a real reason for listening. Otherwise, the listening instructions may be heard as just the usual teacher rhetoric.

## STEP 3:
## GIVING THE INTRODUCTIONS

Allow the students to use their notes to introduce each other to the whole class. As the students are introduced, with a big round of applause for each person, followed by the listeners' responses, the teacher (or a student volunteer) records on the blackboard or on a flip chart the places of origin inside and outside the United States, and dates of immigration to the local city. The list will be a mixture of town and city names, states, regions, continents, and foreign countries. Don't worry too much if it's not exact, for you and the students will refine it later. This list will be a key tool in moving from the introductions to the more extended history and geography curriculum of the project.

Allow plenty of time for the Getting to Know You Culturally workshop to be completed. It gets things off to a good start, and each person is given a moment to shine. Some of the pressure is off because each student is introducing someone else. Yet as the list of origin places grows, it gains in richness, mystery, and intrigue. *Everyone comes from somewhere. Every family arrived here at some time.* What are these places? What caused these journeys? The list of arrival dates will be short at first, but as data are brought in later, the trends that appear will invite questions that can be explored as part of your curriculum.

## STEP 4:
## FILLING THE INFORMATION GAPS AT HOME

Students will be unable to answer some of the questions during the interview. For homework, they are instructed to take home the list of unanswered questions to ask their parents, extended family members, or guardians. To help focus the information, have each interviewer ask for more information on one aspect of the partner's background that she's especially curious about. The next day, students will share the new information they've gathered with the person who interviewed them, who will then add to the previous data in preparation for writing a descriptive piece about their partner.

## STEP 5:
## COMPOSING PARTNER PORTRAITS

It's in the language arts that students are doing the heavy lifting, here in the beginning of the project, even though we're setting things up to pose many questions for social studies. Once students have brought in their families' answers to their questions, they can go to work writing a one-page introduction about their partner. Depending on the age and preparation of the students, you may need to provide some steps and models for this work. Help students think and talk for a few minutes about how they might organize their information. Younger children usually tend to use a question-and-answer format, or to simply list information in the order they heard it or remembered it, rather than in any logical sequence. Students can be asked to look over their information, pick one key item or focus on the one aspect of their partner's background they asked about, and jot a few notes on why it stands out.

Rather than simply listing the data, it's useful if students can find a theme or key fact that connects with their central impression of the person. Another way to help with this is to create a model by writing an introduction of yourself, as if observed by someone else, place it on an overhead transparency, and discuss it with your students. Better yet, place just a list of facts about yourself on the overhead, and have the students help find the key item that unifies a portrait of you. Mini-lessons on leads or conclusions are also relevant here. Adding up all the cultural facts, what overall impression of his or her partner has the writer gained? How can a statement about this be turned into a good beginning or ending sentence for the piece? Finding a core, a theme, a thread that makes sense of information is a challenging task, especially for younger students, so it's a skill you may want to work on repeatedly during the project.

After completing a writing strategy mini-lesson, allow about thirty minutes of in-class writing workshop time, during which you circulate and conference briefly with students who need help (see Chapter 4, "Writing and Other Forms of Expression in Family History"). When students are preparing their final drafts, instruct them to leave space in the top corner to attach the photograph you have had developed.

If you have access to a copying machine, you can make copies of the resulting class portrait book for each student. If not, the original book can be displayed for students to look over, which they will do eagerly.

## goals and objectives

By the end of this session, some amazing and important things will have happened:

- ◆ The students have realized they are the focus of inquiry, the source of information, and the researchers.
- ◆ Each student has been honored for the unique history he or she brings to the class.
- ◆ Each student has had the opportunity to speak before the whole group and gain confidence in doing so.
- ◆ A wealth of information has been gathered for use in creating

a classroom profile that will be reflected on, referred to, and developed through research and literature during the whole unit.

- Students have learned to give focus to and organize information.
- Each student has completed a one-page written piece about another student.
- A sense of classroom community has been established and celebrated.

## what we got—reality checks

Figure 2.1 shows Manal Ghouleh's write-up of an interview with classmate Daniel Quick in Sharon West's third-grade class at Hurley School. Another of Sharon's students, Beatrice Garza, wrote the following interview portrait of Baraah Ghouleh, which is also discussed in Chapter 4:

### Beatrice Garza, Hurley School, Room 302

Hi, my name is Beatrice Garza. The school I go to is Hurley Elementary. I am Mexican American. I interviewed Baraah Ghouleh. She is named after no one. The language spoken in her home is Arabic. Her name means innocent. She was born in Chicago. She was born in 1990. Her parents came from Palestine. She lived out of the U.S. when she was little. I was surprised that her favorite food is humus. Humus is smashed beans. I discovered that there was a holiday called Eid. She also celebrates Ramadan. It is a whole month of fasting. They stop eating at sunrise till sunset, and then get together as a big family for fotor. Her mom makes all kinds of food, like humus, macloupe, mansaf, mosakan, and a bunch of sweets, like katay and hareseh and other kinds of sweets, and at the end of the month they celebrate Eid by going to the mosque. They wear Jillbab and they have to cover their heads with scarfs. I was surprised that her dad was her hero. Her dad is her hero because he does things for her. I discovered that the clothing worn is called Jillbab. Jillbab is the women's clothing. She likes humus because it is smashed beans. She speaks English and Arabic. I really liked doing this project.

   hareseh: flower, water, and oil mixed with powder
   katyif: pancakes, nuts, sugar, and syrup

Manal Ghouleh       November 9, 1998
Hurley School        302-3
        Hi, My name is Manal
Ghouleh. I intervied Daniel Quick. He
told me how his family celebrates
Easter in Greece. Daniel told me a
game that his family and him play
at Easter time. Frist they color
the eggs red. Second his family
puts the egg in there hand. Third
they try to not to brake
their egg. The one who cracks
the egg loses.

        Daniel and his family celebrate
Greek Easter. They celebrate it
because it is the day Jesus rose
from the dead. The family colors
the egg red because of Jecu's
blood. When they get ready to
crack the egg they say creistos
sthestos it means christ has
risin. That is how they celebrate
Greek Easter.

        Daniel Quick is Greek
Amercan. He is 9 years old. His
favorite food is feta cheese. His
favorite subject is school is
Science. Daniel like to play games.
He was born 1989. His faroite sport
is football.

FIGURE 2.1
Manal Ghouleh interviews Daniel Quick

macloupe: a meal that has rice with cleaned meat or chicken,
    potatoes, carrots, and egg plant
mansaf: bread, meat, rice, and yogurt
mosakan: bread, chicken, onions, and red spices

## WORKING WITH PARENTS

A group of parents at Jenner Academy, in the Cabrini-Green housing complex, generated a list of origin places only to find that 90 percent of them were in Mississippi. We had big maps on hand so people
who knew their exact hometowns could mark them. By compiling a list
of migration dates, grouping them by decade, and creating bar graphs,
we reproduced the migration surges of the twentieth century. Later we
watched the film *Goin' to Chicago*, which gives the historical context of the
great migration from the South.

During the next few weeks, as parents continued to bring in family
documents with place names listed, we frequently used the atlases to
find obscure hometowns. Extended family members were tapped for information about how things were back in the old days, down south.

This work on family history with parents fed into a schoolwide focus on the subject. Pat Bearden helped the third- through eighth-grade
teachers create a format for students to bring in family information—
family obituaries, pictures, documents, and keepsakes. Tracey Cunningham, the third-grade teacher, guided her students in compiling a classroom profile. Kids in all classes wrote essays about family members. The
principal, Sandra Satinover, created her own chart with family pictures.
Keepsakes included an uncle's helmet from World War II, family Bibles,
and a buffalo-head nickel with a story behind it. Teachers brought in
their own treasured objects, such as family quilts passed down from
grandmothers. The art teacher helped students put it all together on
stand-up posterboards, and at the end of the year, the school held a family history fair (see Figure 2.2). Along with the kids' displays, Pat set up a
literature table with history books on various periods, time-line books,
picture books, historical fiction, and nonfiction. Time lines tracing Chicago and U.S. history were put up on walls; parents put up family time
lines and placed their own displays alongside kids'. The fair stayed up
through graduation, and kids still talk about last year's fair.

FIGURE 2.2
The Family History Fair at McDowell School

# CHAPTER 3
## *Family interview and classroom profile*

urley School third-grade teacher Sharon West observes, "The most important thing I'm finding out about the family history project is that it opens doors at home. In lots of families, there isn't much conversation. This project gets communication started." During the last workshop, when your students did the Pair-Share Interview, they probably were not able to answer all the questions about their background on their own, so they took their questions home to get answers from their families. During this workshop, students will complete a new, more in-depth questionnaire at their most important source of information, their home, with the help of parents, guardian, and/or extended family.

The Classroom Profile Questionnaire invites students to tap into the wealth of knowledge across the dinner table. When kids bring the questionnaire home, it creates a new reason for dialogue among family members. It causes photographs to get strewn all over the living room floor. It causes sticky bottom drawers to be unstuck to reveal their rich contents of legal documents and memorabilia. In the process, students learn and practice techniques for interviewing, note taking, and synthesizing information.

Back at school, the classroom profile workshop serves a variety of important purposes:

♦ To draw students' attention to the similarities and diversities within their own classroom.
♦ To highlight facts and patterns that will later connect with national history and geography.

◆ To learn skills for analyzing and graphing data.

◆ To continue to build and deepen trust and create a community of learners in the classroom.

The questions that guide students' data gathering will focus on the ethnic groups represented; who, when, where, and why their relatives and ancestors migrated to their current home; the jobs they held along the way; and the wars, social struggles, and political developments in which their relatives played a part. This information offers a personal platform for students to learn, discuss, and write about the *historical events, core democratic values, fundamental beliefs,* and *governmental principles* that are such an important part of social studies.

The students will assemble this treasure trove of historical materials as the primary source of their collective inquiry. Then they will work in teams to compile the collected information, to sort it, tabulate it, graph it, present it to the whole group, and reflect on its significance. Increasingly, the students will find that they are learning from one another, and each will begin to realize that his or her family's experiences are valuable to others. The resulting charts and graphs will remain posted around the classroom as an evolving display of group self-identification and a source of further analysis and link between students' families and the stuff of the social studies curriculum.

In addition to connecting with the official curriculum, the project will gradually open up more and more to student choice and initiative. If the best national curriculum standards advise us to make learning more student-centered and authentic, then we must make sure the family history project does that. Some teachers and observers of American education imagine that giving students choice and initiative means "letting kids do whatever they want" and abandoning our role as teachers. We've found, however, that students can begin making thoughtful and effective choices about what to learn and how to investigate if they possess sufficient prior knowledge about a subject, *or* if they receive sufficient guidance and structures for gaining that prior knowledge. The role of the teacher, in other words, is crucial in making student-centered learning really work.

The group and individual activities of the project thus far are mainly structured by the teacher, who decides to focus on family history, asks students to interview each other, gives out questionnaires, sends kids home to gather data, and organizes groups to compile the results. However, once the data begin coming in, things grow less predictable and more dependent on what students find and what aspects of their family history they are most interested in. Wonderful surprises turn up, and you, the teacher, will be drawn to helping and encouraging students to follow their leads.

# how-to guide
## STEP 1:
## PREPARE STUDENTS TO GATHER MORE DATA

Pass out the following Classroom Profile Questionnaire to your students and help them prepare to go through it with their families.

## Classroom Profile Questions

1. Describe your ethnic background.
2. When did your people first come to this place where we live?
3. Who were the first family members to come here?
4. Where did they come from? (state, city, and/or country in/outside the United States)
5. Why did they leave their former home?
6. Why did they come to this place?
7. What types of jobs did they get when they arrived?
8. What jobs did they have before they came here?
9. In which wars or struggles did any of your relatives play a part?
10. Ask follow-up questions on the topics about which your parent or guardian shows the most interest.

### Interviewing Mini-Lesson—Teacher Self-Interview

It is essential to do more than just hand the questionnaire to students for homework. You can prepare students in a variety of ways to effectively gather answers to these questions at home so their efforts have the highest probability of success. No matter what their age or achievement level, students new to this primary-source research need many skills so they can do it well. A good way to start is to share your own family story with the students as you use an overhead projector to fill in your answers to the questions. Illustrate how to use a key strategy such as asking follow-up questions, by first giving short, limited bits of information and then inviting students to ask you more about each item. If students are new to this, you may need to pose a few such questions yourself.

### Interviewing Mini-Lesson—Role Play

To prepare your students for the actual interview process, have them *role play* in pairs an imaginary interview session with their parents. A good way to get the role plays going is to have every pair in the class practice their own role play first, with one student asking the other one questions and the other pretending to be a parent. Then, based on your own observations, choose two or three illustrative pairs to reenact their role play for the whole class. Before the role plays are practiced, however, briefly explain strategies for good interviewing that can help family members overcome their hesitation to talk about themselves:

- ◆ Using techniques to help the interviewed person and the interviewer relax.
- ◆ Using follow-up questions for clarification.
- ◆ Avoiding yes-no questions ("fat" versus "skinny" questions).
- ◆ Recognizing topics that require consulting someone else in the family.
- ◆ Dealing with sensitive topics that require tact or may need to be dropped.

As the role plays are presented, ask the rest of the students to watch for and then comment on the strategies they observe. As you proceed with this exercise, help your students understand the importance of respecting privacy and how it balances with a child's desire and right to know his or her family history. It is essential to assure your students that with proper respect and patience on the part of the student-interviewer, most parents become enthusiastic storytellers and investigators into their own past.

### Interviewing Mini-Lesson—Note taking

Unless urged otherwise, many students will cling to the belief that they can just listen to their interviewee and remember all that is said. To help with note-taking skills, model on the overhead your own note taking, jotting of small bits of information, abbreviations, and personal shorthand for keeping up with the flow of conversation. Students can then practice taking notes while one or several volunteers relate family facts or events they've already learned about. In pairs and in the whole group, students can compare what they chose to jot down, what they omitted as unnecessary, and how they abbreviated the information. If the equipment is available, you can also discuss and demonstrate the benefits and liabilities of using tape or video recorders during the interviews.

## Vocabulary

During your mini-lessons on interviewing, you may find your students need to learn related vocabulary. For example, our *ancestors* are those who lived before us, and our *relatives* are those who live today. One handy way to address this need is to start a *word wall* in a prominent place in the classroom so that your students become familiar with these important words.

A *word wall* is a bulletin board space you prepare, where you gradually add new vocabulary words and work with them over time. Direct students to consult them when reading and writing, and use games and activities to review and deepen students' vocabulary knowledge as you work through the family history project. Examples of vocabulary games:

- Wordo—Students fill in a bingo-type chart as you call out word definitions.
- Word Sorts—Students sort and list words from the wall based on various criteria you offer, focused either on letter and sound patterns or on aspects of word meaning.
- Mind Reader—Give clues and have students write down the word once they've guessed it (thus everyone participates rather than one winner calling out the answer).

(For more on these and other word-level strategies, see Patricia Cunningham, *Phonics They Use,* and Camille Blachowicz and Peter Fisher, *Teaching Vocabulary in All Classrooms.*)

As you prepare the students for this work, emphasize that

- We all have ancestors. That is how we came to be here.
- We all have families. They come in different forms.
- We all have stories. They are unique to us.
- We all come from somewhere. There are stories embedded in these journeys.
- Our family stories help to make public history.

## STEP 2:
## SUPPORT WHILE STUDENTS ARE INTERVIEWING

As your students take the questionnaire home to interview their parents or guardians, make sure everyone understands the directions. Mention that it is important for everyone in the class to participate to ensure a broad sample and real representation. Students should try to get every question answered. For example, if only one child answers the question about his or her family's participation in wars and struggles, the class profile will suggest 100 percent participation or nonparticipation, but this will not be an accurate statistical representation of the whole class. It's advisable to send a letter home with students to explain the project to their parents or other family members, to encourage their participation, and to assure them that concerns for privacy will be respected. A sample letter is included with the Reality Checks for this chapter.

Considering parents' work schedules and other interruptions, your students may need a few days to complete the interview. They may need to talk to other relatives. Parents need time, too, to consider these questions and to retrieve documents and photos. Some questions take weeks and months for answers to trickle in. The Classroom Profile Questionnaire will continue to yield information throughout the school year, but the bulk of the questions can be answered in a short period of time. Give the process a few days, but set a deadline to work toward.

To help make sure work doesn't lag, it is a good idea to hold an occasional *status of the class* session. In *status of the class* (best described by Nancie Atwell in *In the Middle: New Understandings About Writing, Reading, and Learning*), all students in the class share orally in just a brief phrase or two how the interviews are going and what problems may have arisen. This not only gives you a quick picture of how the work is proceeding and who may need extra help, it also encourages students who are procrastinating to get started so they won't be put on the spot when you repeat your survey in a day or two. You can also ask students who have successfully answered some questions to share them in more depth with the class. Journals are extremely helpful for supporting and monitoring the research process. Allow time for everyone to write in his or her journal about the successes and/or obstacles they encountered in their inquiry. Delays aren't necessarily the students' fault, and the journals will provide you with insight about what might be impeding a student's progress.

## STEP 3:
## CONNECTING WITH LITERATURE

While the family interview process is brewing, you can heighten interest, make connections across the curriculum, and further emphasize the role of individual families in national history by introducing your students to literature that describes different types of families in migration from place to place. It's especially powerful to read short picture books or excerpts of longer chapter books aloud. Here are a few samples:

That night, all of Mama's children were assembled together for the last time on earth. The next day Bob and Sarah went back to Jacksonville to school. Papa was away from home a great deal, so two weeks later, I was on my way to Jacksonville, too. I was under age but the school had agreed to take me in under the circumstances. My sister was to look after me, in a way.

The midnight train had to be waved down at Maitland for me. That would put me into Jacksonville in the daytime.

—from *Dust Tracks on a Road*, Zora Neale Hurston

I had gone from job to job, working at the cotton mill, and all that, having Donna Lee and Vince and working in the mill to raise them. I'd just had it up to here. So I just made up my mind that I was going to get away from that mill village. I said I wanted to go as far as I could get without getting out of the United States.

Well, this taxi driver I'd been dating, and this other taxi driver and his girl friend, they said to me about one o'clock on a Friday afternoon, they said, "Let's go to the State of Washington." And I said, "By, God, I'm game!" They said "You're chickenshit. You won't go." I said, "Hell, I will go." I went home and I said, "Mama. I'm leaving. Will you keep the kids till I get a job and a place to live? Then I'll send for them or come back and get them. Mama said yes. I packed my little suitcase and at four o'clock they picked me up and we were on our way."

—from *Hillbilly Women*, Kathy Kahn

"Next week you will be a teeneyer," Papi said as we sat on the porch smelling the night air.

"What's that?"

"In the United States, when children reach the age of thirteen they're called teeneyers. It comes from the ending of the word in English. Thir-teen. Teen-ager."

I counted in English to myself. "So I will be a teeneyer until I am twenty?"

"That's right. Soon you'll be wanting to rock and roll." He laughed as if he had told a very funny joke.

"I don't like rock and roll," I protested. "Too noisy. And it's all in English. I don't understand the songs."

"Mark my words," he said. "When you're a teeneyer it's like something comes over you. Rock and roll sounds good. Believe me." He laughed as if I knew what he was talking about. I hadn't seen him this happy in a long time.

"Well, it's not going to happen to me." I pouted and ignored his chuckles at my expense.

"Just wait," he said. "Once you're in New York, you'll be a regular teeneyer Americana."

"I'm not going to New York."

"Your mother's talking about moving there."

My stomach fell to my feet. "What?"

—from *When I Was Puerto Rican*, Esmerelda Santiago

Following are some additional books on the migration of various ethnic groups:

*The Keeping Quilt*, Patricia Polacco
*Who Belongs Here? An American Story*, Margy Burns Knight
*The Great Migration*, Jacob Lawrence

Allow a chunk of time for students to respond in their journals to the literature after you read each selection.

With a little extra planning, you can connect the family history project with other parts of your curriculum. Using the school library or your own classroom library, gather together fiction and nonfiction books about migrations and the time periods represented by the Classroom Profiles. Encourage students to choose these for independent DEAR time (Drop Everything And Read). If you can obtain multiple copies, you can also make the books available for literature circles, student-led reading/ discussion groups.

## STEP 4:
## COMPILING AND GRAPHING THE DATA

Once the Profile Questionnaires have been substantially completed (don't wait for every detail or you'll lose momentum), explain the objective for the next step: by compiling information from the whole class, patterns and surprising results will reveal themselves. First, have students brainstorm different ways to summarize and display their compiled findings. Then demonstrate, using an overhead projector, how tables, pie charts, and various types of bar graphs are used to describe information. Select one question from the profile and use it to tally and display student responses in a variety of ways.

Now group your students into small teams. Each team is responsible for tabulating *their group profile and* tabulating one or two specific questions for the *whole classroom*. Specific tasks can be assumed by individuals in the teams. One person might take the summarized team results and report them to the other teams. One person can do the graphing, one the mathematical calculations. Several should share the responsibility for giving the presentation. In the early grades, the teacher may need to work in a whole-classroom setting to help children compile the results.

The teams compile findings and summarize trends and patterns that emerge. If students have covered the needed math skills, decimals or percentages should be used to describe, analyze, graph, and chart findings. If it's appropriate for your grade level, you may choose to provide instruction on using x-y coordinates on a graph and measuring the angles to mark off sectors for a pie chart. Provide examples and have the class do practice versions of these, using simple data such as eye color or age groupings of students in the class. Once students begin group work to compile their classroom profile data, the teacher's task is to *observe, coach, assist,* and *prod* the teams to keep the process on track.

Teams then present their results to the class. After the groups report, their findings should be posted in prominent places around the classroom. These provide the basis for the curriculum that *emerges* from the family history project. The teacher can look at these findings, think about the goals and standards that he or she is responsible for during the year, and use the students' own historical data as the jumping off place for accomplishing those goals.

## STEP 5:
## MAKING CONNECTIONS

It is difficult to give precise guidance for this step. The aim now is to begin making connections between the data your students bring in and one or more key elements of the social studies curriculum you must teach. What you focus on will depend on what your students discover and what topics or concepts are listed by your district for the particular grade you teach. However, we can offer examples of the kinds of connections teachers have uncovered. Sharon West of Hurley School describes how one student discovered an ancestor who almost rode on the *Titanic's* fateful voyage, but decided against it at the last minute. The student had not previously known about this famous piece of American history (this was before the movie was made!). The student, now older, continues to return to Sharon's class to report to the younger kids on his further family history discoveries.

In another school, working with a group of adults, Pat and Yolanda probed for additional connections by passing out *name dictionaries* during the interview pair-share. One woman sat transfixed by the information she discovered about her surname, Weiss. It seems that in the Middle Ages, the Germans who ruled eastern Russia divided up the Jewish population for taxation purposes. They described one group as *Weiss* (light skinned), one group *Schwartz* (dark), one group *Klein* (small), and another group *Gross* (big, or fat). Thus she discovered that the history of these common Jewish surnames is linked to the oppression of Jews in Europe centuries ago. Tears flowed, were shared by her interview partners, and finally by the whole group.

As teachers, we watch for opportunities to connect with the formal curriculum as well—though we must be sure to make these connections real and meaningful, and not just thinly veiled leaps to whatever comes next on the district standards list. Here are a few examples.

### Connecting with the Formal Curriculum—Geography

When Pat Bearden realized her students had been repeatedly returning to the classroom map with pins that showed where all the students' families were from, she recognized an opportunity to capitalize on their interest and teach some geography by devising a game she and the students called Origins. She divided the students into two teams, and the teams took turns finding places of origin identified in the classroom profile. In addition to finding the location on a U.S. or world map, the students were asked to identify longitude and latitude, the continent, hemisphere, and land regions of the given location. Each group member took a turn, ensuring full participation. This game quickly became a class favorite.

### Connecting with the Formal Curriculum—Math

Producing a pie chart for analyzing and presenting the classroom profile will involve students in arithmetic, calculating percentages, and graphing. Depending on the time available, the direction that the class inquiry is taking, and the teacher's mathematics goals, other tasks can be assigned, such as averaging, estimation, and so on. For example, if students question how extensively wars affected the lives of families, the teacher can show how to extrapolate from their own classroom to the larger population. If seventeen out of thirty-two students find that a relative has fought in one of the major twentieth-century wars, students first calculate the percentage this represents—53.1 percent. If this class is similar to the whole population, how many of the country's 270 million people have a relative who has been involved in one of the wars? (That is, what is 53.1 percent of 270,000,000?) What is the probability that a new student will have a participating relative?

### Connecting with the Formal Curriculum—History

History is for many reasons full of wars, conflict, and struggles. By starting with the data from the classroom profile, students can be helped to begin investigating one of these conflicts with a real sense of its impact on their own families, or the families of their friends. Students can then embark on investigations about the reasons for it; write about someone's experience during it; and read novels set in it (*Fallen Angels*, Walter Dean Myers—Vietnam War; *For Whom the Bell Tolls*, Ernest Hemingway—Spanish Civil War; *Farewell to Manzanar*, Jeanne Wakatsuki Houston, and *Anne Frank: Diary of a Young Girl*—World War II). A teacher with the goal of covering World War II during the school year, for example, could use the chart on whose ancestors and relatives fought in wars as a way to enter into the subject. What are the current ages of these participants? If they were in their early twenties when they went to war, about when were they born? Are they still living and available for interview or to speak to the class? What kind of work were they doing before and after the war? For a classroom to share this kind of information—that their relatives were involved and sacrificed themselves—builds self-esteem and a sense of belonging, and it places students and their families in public history. (See the Reality Checks in Chapter 6 for an example of how one junior high teacher team used such connections in an extensive multidisciplinary unit.)

## goals and objectives

At the end of this process, your students have had an important, validating interchange in the home. They have learned and practiced techniques for note taking and interviewing. They have activated in themselves and their families the curiosity that arises from unanswered questions. They've used their journal to reflect on the inquiry process itself, and shared roadblocks with their classmates.

Back in the classroom they worked collaboratively to collect and sort information, and used higher-order thinking skills to connect and compare data, find mathematical ways to render and present information, and share their findings with fellow students, using graphic presentational methods.

The classroom and teacher are rewarded with a profile of the class, a distinctive form created by highlighting the unique contours of a data set. Often, some striking, unusual, and interesting patterns reveal themselves. If teachers keep their educational goals in mind, they will immediately begin to see the possibilities for linking profiles and curriculum through activities in mathematics, literature, art, writing, geography, and more.

The students have been exposed to a wide range of multicultural literature and nonfiction books about peoples and their migrations. They have selected and responded to books of their own choice and started to make connections between their own family history and the public history represented in books.

Thus, by the end of this portion of the project, your class will have accomplished the following:

◆ Learned and practiced interviewing strategies.
◆ Learned and used note-taking strategies.
◆ Learned to persevere in gathering research information.
◆ Learned skills for analyzing and presenting data.
◆ Worked cooperatively in groups.
◆ Been exposed to significant multicultural literature.
◆ Learned facts about diverse and similar backgrounds of students in the class.

The Classroom Profile is not a static artifact. It can grow throughout the year as new information is gathered. It can be referred to time and time again. The means to accomplishing educational goals emerges from the *inquiry process* initiated by the classroom profile and your students' search into their own family histories. Because students become highly engaged in this process, many will continue to pursue the search on their own, long after you've formally completed the family history project.

# reality checks
## DOING THE INTERVIEWS—HURLEY SCHOOL THIRD GRADE

Here's a sample of the responses to some of the profile questions obtained by one student in Sharon West's third-grade class at Hurley Elementary School in Chicago. This initial information is sketchy, but as the class begins to compile information, it gains more shape and

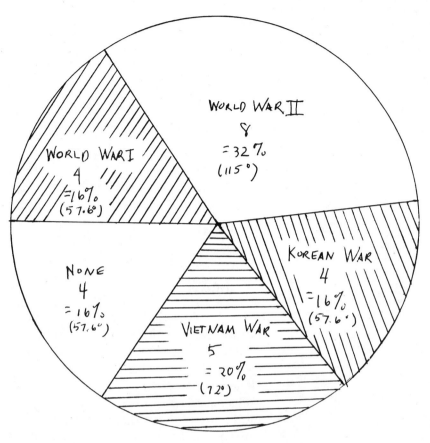

FIGURE 3.1
Ancestors who fought in wars—pie chart from Hurley School, Third Grade

significance, as you can see from the pie chart in Figure 3.1, which shows their relatives' participation in wars during this century.

## Sample Family Interview Responses

1. What is your ethnic makeup?

   *Maternal grandparents Mexican. Maternal great-grandparents Italian and Spanish.*

2. When did your people first come to Chicago?

   *Sept. 25, 1976.*

3. Who were the first family members to come to Chicago?

   *Grandma Elba Trejo, Grandpa Mariano Trejo, and my Aunt Olivia.*

4. Where did they come from?

*Ixtapaluca in the state of Mexico.*

5. Why did they come to Chicago?

*To save money to build a house for my mother and uncles.*

6. What types of jobs did they get when they arrived?

*My grandfather worked in a warehouse where they stored all kinds of nuts. He also worked in a cookie factory with my grandmother.*

7. What jobs did they have before they came to Chicago?

*My grandfather worked in a paper company and my grandmother was a housewife.*

8. What wars did your relatives serve in?

*None that we know of.*

### DOWN SOUTH

At McDowell Elementary School on Chicago's South Side, Adrienne Brown-Murray's fifth-grade class took home their classroom profile and within a few days the information started to come in. They produced the chart in Figure 3.2 showing the class's origins in the southern part of the United States, reflecting the school's African American community. The profile raised many questions: Why were African Americans clustered in the South? Why did they leave? When? Are there any historical novels depicting the areas of the South listed here? What kinds of work did they do for a living in the South? In Chicago? The teacher used local library resources to find history books and stories that helped students learn answers to these questions, and the students dove into them as part of the reading program.

This is the same class that is described in the introduction, however, and when the kids discovered their many connections to famous people, Mrs. Brown-Murray was happy to allow additional time to pursue that side of the project as well.

### PAT BEARDEN'S CLASSROOM: HOW THE CLASSROOM PROFILE EXPANDS NATURALLY

Pat's story:

When I tried for the first time leading my students through the creation of a class profile on family history, my students made the following list of places where they were born:

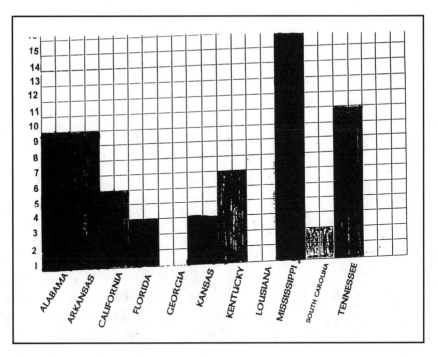

**FIGURE 3.2**

Graph of places of family origin from McDowell School, Fifth Grade

## Origins Within the United States

| | |
|---|---|
| Alabama | Arkansas |
| Kansas | Louisiana |
| Minnesota | Tennessee |
| Texas | Mississippi |

## Origins Outside the United States

| | |
|---|---|
| Africa | El Salvador |
| Finland | India |
| Italy | Mexico |
| North America | Pakistan |
| Puerto Rico | Trinidad |

A list of origin sites such as this creates a whole new reason for having good maps in a classroom—and using them. Notice that the entry "North America" is honored although it is vague in the extreme. All of these responses called for new questions:

- ◆ Where in North America?
- ◆ Where in Puerto Rico?
- ◆ Where in Africa?
- ◆ Is it possible to find these answers?
- ◆ What events of history brought all these stories to our school?

As we clarified the answers, I created a bulletin board with photos I'd taken of each of the students, arranged around a world map. Using pushpins, I stretched a string from each photo to the student's family's place of origin on the map. This visual representation heightened the children's interest markedly. In fact, as we moved further into the project, I noticed that this class, which had many behavior problems, was growing calmer and more respectful of one another. The whole tone in the classroom seemed to change.

This inspired me to introduce additional activities. I paired students to do additional interviews of each other to compare the cultures they came from, and to identify ways that different cultures were similar and different. When this, too, worked well, I thought, Let's keep going! I asked the children each to interview an adult in the building about his or her culture. This in turn incited interest among the rest of the faculty, and we decided to create our own teachers' bulletin board in a prominent hallway, with pictures, a map, pins, and strings to show places of origin. The kids, of course, were fascinated.

Next, I decided to extend the focus on cultural heritage by asking the kids, "Who are your heroes?" I received these answers:

| | |
|---|---|
| Dr. King | Benito Juarez |
| Sitting Bull | Cochise |
| Jesse Jackson | Harold Washington |
| Pancho Villa | Harriet Tubman |
| Emilio Zapata | Malcolm X |
| Haile Selassie | |

I'd received a small grant from the Oppenheimer Family Foundation to build up my classroom library, and I decided to purchase books on these historical and political figures so the students could learn about them in more depth during sustained silent reading time, within the reading program. I had no difficulty maintaining kids' interest in reading on this topic.

Finally, for a culminating activity, I asked students to write essays about their cultural heritages, using knowledge they had gained from both their family history investigations and from the books on their cultural heroes. The students proudly presented the finished book of their essays, titled, *All About Me and My Heritage*, to the foundation director.

## A MIDDLE SCHOOL CLASS FOCUSES ON THE INTERVIEW

Eighth-grade teacher Jane Sanders Boyce, at Hebron Middle School in Hebron, Indiana, has for four years been asking students to interview family members during the Christmas holiday, and then to write about one ancestor or living relative. Rather than compile interview data into a profile, she concentrates simply on helping students elaborate and refine their interview piece. Jane reflects on the project:

> I will confess that I had some misgivings when I first gave this assignment. So many of my students tell me in various ways that they have no real family, or that they don't ever see them much if they do have them. Mom or Dad either live somewhere else, or they work the afternoon shift and are "never home." Dad disappeared three years ago, and we're not allowed to ask about him. My stepgranddad doesn't really know us, or like us. . . . As I read over my students' work, doing the teacher edit conference before their final "publication" (the pieces have already gone through two revisions before I see them), I am amazed at the stories I am reading. Maybe it's the subject matter, or maybe it's the very open and honest nature of middle school students, but I feel that the quality of these stories is higher than any I've had all year. There is a real sense of celebration involved with each one; my students are very anxious to show their written work to their peers and to me. They are eager to see my reaction to their stories, and I have even caught them sitting in peer revision groups getting "off the subject" of their written stories, because they are telling their friends the rest of the stories they know, the ones they haven't written down yet!

One student's interview piece:

### Grandma's Life

I asked my grandma to tell me a story of her life for my family history book. I asked her to tell me about what school was like. I asked her to tell me about the things that she did. I asked her about the games that she played. They would look through other people's windows to watch T.V. They bought their food and coal off trucks that would come by their house.

I asked my grandma to tell me about her childhood.

She told me that they would walk to school and play games like ball and jacks, hide and seek, eenie inie over, kick the can, dominoes, pick up sticks, tag and jump rope. They roller skated on the sidewalk with metal clamp-on skates.

Then I asked her about school. She told me that they never had a school cafeteria and that in elementary you either carried lunch or walked home if you lived close enough to the school. The school was a big two story building that had a fire escape that you slid down. In the summertime the kids would play on it and use wax paper to slide down it.

"We played a lot of baseball on the field on the playground."

Next, she told me that they used to pick cherries and sell them around the neighborhood in a wagon in the summertime. When T.V.'s first came out only one family on the block had one. All of the kids would stand on their porch and look at it through their window.

"Before we got a refrigerator we had an icebox and the iceman brought big blocks of ice two to three times a week and he carried them with metal tongs."

"We heated the house with a coal furnace."

There was a coal bin in the basement and the coal man dumped coal through a window in the basement wall. The house would be very cold in the mornings in the wintertime until the fire got stoked.

"We would stand over the floor registers to keep warm."

Then she told me about what the farmers did in the summertime. She said that the farmers would drive their trucks by the houses yelling, "Vegetables for sale—potatoes, corn, beans, apples, pears, peaches, carrots," and the people would come out of their houses and buy the vegetables off the truck. She also said that whenever there was important news like the war ending, a presidential election, a major crisis, or something big there would be special editions of the newspaper and paperboys would be out on the sidewalks yelling, "Extra, extra read all about it."

She told me about the time that president Truman came to Muskegon on the caboose of a train. The school kids were dismissed to walk to the train station and see him. She also said that in Muskegon there were many special parades on special days like Easter, Christmas, Thanksgiving, 4th of July, and memorial Day.

"All of this happened between 1947 and 1952 when I lived across the street from the school in Muskegon, Michigan."

I learned that they had a hard life compared to what we have. We have a lot of appliances that they didn't have that would have been helpful to them.

In spite of a few bumps in her prose, this student's attentive and engaged piece shows us how a wide variety of information gives depth and richness to such a portrait.

An important final step in the project for Jane Sanders Boyce is to ask students to reflect on what they've learned. This provides us with perhaps the most powerful evidence about why such a project is needed in classrooms today. Following is a sampling of typical responses:

- I have pride and respect for certain people who fought in wars and survived. That takes a whole lot of guts.
- I am both Italian and German—I have the best of both worlds!
- I learned that my mom had funny stories that she never told me before.
- I have the feeling that my grandma and my uncle both loved to help me. I was very proud and overwhelmed with their help.
- I think my family is a very brave family. When I called my grandma she was very happy that I was learning about my family.
- I am proud that my grandmother still carries all her culture from Sweden.
- When I called my grandma I could tell she was excited about me calling.
- When I called my grandmother long distance, we were on the phone for over an hour because she had so much to say.
- My grandma told me that every Christmas her dad would go to the bars and take all the servicemen and let them eat Christmas dinner with them. He was a good man.
- I understand why my family doesn't yell at us for a lot of things, because they did them too when they were little.
- I learned why people say respect your elders.
- I really respect my mom now, because I know she was my age once and made mistakes too.
- I wish I could meet my ancestors so they could tell me how it was and how they felt.

- ◆ I respect my ancestors that fought in the wars the most because they risked their lives for their country.
- ◆ I learned that my ancestor signed the Polish constitution.
- ◆ I now wish I would live up to the courage my ancestors had.
- ◆ My grandma told me all about World War I and the Great Depression.
- ◆ My mom told me about my great-grandparents' farm. Now I can picture it.
- ◆ Now that I've written them down, I can share these stories and keep them forever.
- ◆ My great-great-grandfather was part of the underground railroad and that makes me proud.
- ◆ My family was glad to help me, especially my grandpa. Once you got him going, he'd never quit.
- ◆ I am glad I found out about all my great-grandparents. My family feels more complete.

## A HIGH SCHOOL FAMILY STORY

At the Best Practice High School, in Chicago, Tina Peano's junior English classes found themselves in a sharp debate on whether it was preferable to put aside the past so it would not weigh a person down, or to examine it to understand it better. To help them explore the issue and find value in their family's wisdom, Tina asked everyone to identify and recount a "story to grow up on," that is, a story, event, or struggle they'd been told from their own family's past. Many of the stories were obtained through interviews with parents, whereas others reflected more ongoing interchanges within the family. Jose's story covers, in its own natural course, nearly all the questions from the Classroom Profile Questionnaire.

When I was twelve years old my mother and I had just come home from picking up my report card at Irma C. Ruiz School. I had "A's" two "B's" and two "C's." My dad was disappointed at me that I shouldn't be getting "C's" not even "B's," he said that there was no reason for me to get those grades. He asked me if I knew how to do all the work in school, if I understand it. I answered yes, and that's when everything began. As soon as I answered yes he started giving a lecture.

The first thing he said was that when he was in school he used to get 10's. A 10 was an "A" since he used to live in Mexico and he went to school over there. He said that it was harder back then to study because everything they had to do they had to do it on their own, no calculators no nothing, they barely had paper and pens. We come from a small town in Mexico so there it was hard to get materials. He said that we have everything easy here that technology helps us learn and that we don't take advantage of that. One thing was leading to another until he said, "That's why I came here, to this country, so you my children didn't have to suffer like I did. But you don't want it, you just want to fool around. What would you do if this keeps going, today is a 'C,' tomorrow a 'D' until it does down to an 'F.' Do you want to live like me, to work at a factory or do you want to have a good job where you don't need to use your back and you have to use your head, to get good money so you don't have to worry about anything?" When my father said that it started to open my eyes but I still didn't care, I was just twelve years old, all I wanted to do was play. My dad saw that somehow he knew that he was getting through my head but that I still didn't care so he got serious and he started to tell me a short story of when he got to Chicago.

He started by saying, "When I got married to your mother in Mexico I was working at a place where we fixed the buses." As soon as he finished saying that, I thought *another one of his stories again.* "I worked there until you were 3 years old. I was not getting enough money, I knew that I wanted something else, I wanted to grow to change, I knew that if I stood in that job I was always going to stay the same way. That's when I decided to come to the U.S. to look for an opportunity to be more, to do more. I crossed the border and a friend helped me get here. I was living with eight guys, they were people I knew when I was in Mexico but we had some problems. I wanted to get out, to move out, so I decided to bring your uncle over here." My uncle also crossed the border and he went to live in the same place. I knew that my father was glad to see my uncle here in the U.S. next to him, now he would have some support, especially from his family. "When your uncle got here he started to work the next day at where I was working, in a restaurant."

"When he and I had enough money we moved out. We moved to Montrose and Broadway, it was a small house but it was only us two, we didn't need a big house. We each had two jobs, there were some days that I didn't even see him, our refrigerator was empty, the only thing we ate was McDonald's, Subway and other junk food. We only used the house to sleep. I was saving my money so I could bring your mother and all of you over here. A

year later I told your mom that I had to bring her and Susy first."
Susy is my younger sister, she was one year old at that time. "Your
mother and sister got here and the house was too small so we
moved out to a bigger house at 27th and Ashland. I quit my job at a
restaurant and got the job at the factory, your mom started working
there too. We wanted to raise enough money to bring your sister
and you here so your mom got a job at a building cleaning the
rooms. So now your mom had two jobs."

"It took us nine months to bring you here. When we got the
money we brought you here so we could start a new life." I realized that my dad wanted to give us anything he could to make us
have a better life than the one he did have. He said he didn't want
us to suffer. When he said that my head opened, it was like if I
wanted to study, like if suddenly my life was perfect, I knew what I
wanted and how I was going to do it. . . .

## LETTER FOR PARENTS

Since parental or other adult cooperation is so important to this
project, and particularly to the family surveying and interviewing described in this chapter, most teachers find it essential to send home a letter about the unit. It can inform and prepare the family, and prepares the
way for honoring the occasional request from a family that information
not be sought. Here is one version of the letter Pat Bearden used when
working with the third graders at Hurley School.

Dear Parents, Guardians, and School Community Members:
    In an effort to foster cultural awareness and family participa-
tion in our children's education, we are beginning a family history
research project as a part of the social studies curriculum. Studying
family history promotes critical thinking and inquiry-based learning, which result in deeper understanding of historical concepts
and content. It helps students to identify how their families fit into
public history, so the students can more easily make sense of the
past, find meaning in their world, and eventually see themselves as
a part of world citizenry.
    We will study the life, literature, culture, and the political,
economic, and historical customs of diverse cultures. Our study
begins by learning about the ethnic population represented in our
own classroom, with particular emphasis on how our own family
stories are woven into the fabric of American and global history.

From there, we will use research activities to make connections between our individual cultural backgrounds and public history.

Your cooperation is needed to make the family history project a success. Your child will be interviewing you and other family members. Please take time to help your child complete the family history assignments. Your input is especially important in providing documents, and interviews, and in helping to fill in some of the blanks. Of course, if there is information you are not comfortable sharing, either with your child or with our class, your privacy will be fully respected. However, you can be assured that the information you provide will help your child and the whole class learn more effectively about history, geography, and political science, as well as improve in reading, writing, speaking and listening, and other forms of expression.

Very sincerely,

# CHAPTER 4
## Writing and other forms of expression in family history

*P*owerful and competent writing over a wide variety of genres is a basic goal of every school. And as the first three chapters of this book illustrate, student expression of ideas and information is central to the workings of the family history project. When writing begins with the self, the family, or the community, it provides a medium for inquiry and exploration, it attaches passion and meaning to the practice of writing, and it can produce astonishingly beautiful, important, written history. When Sharon West starts her third graders at Hurley School on a new piece of writing on their family history project, or even when she asks the kids to revise something they've already drafted, no one ever moans or complains. Kids simply get to work and motion eagerly for a visitor to come over to their desks and see what they're doing. In the family history project, students' writing and other forms of expression provide a major, engaging portion of the content that they then analyze, tabulate, and connect with more traditional parts of the school curriculum.

So we pause in the progression of topical sessions in this book to offer some strategies that ensure students' writing in each family history activity is thoroughly developed and of high quality. Teachers who simply announce family history writing topics and send kids home to complete them are likely to be disappointed with what comes back. In contrast, those who provide a good start with plenty of brainstorming, modeling, conversation, and focus lessons on writing strategies, who help students generate choices, who provide in-class writing workshop time, and who conference with individual students while everyone works on their piece, will see great improvements not just in the final products, but in students' skills and knowledge of the writing process. Activities described in this chapter will help teachers incite the kind of powerful, thoughtful, and well-expressed responses that can make the family history project a deep and memorable experience for every student in the room.

And we're not talking just about writing. Art, drama, video, dance, oral presentations, Web site designs—many forms of expression are legitimate, important ways for students to share what they're learning and increase their expressional skills in the process. Indeed, more and more research is revealing how the arts open up academics and literacy for many students who have not been successful in school (see Jeffrey Wilhelm, *You Gotta BE the Book*, and Phyllis Whitin, *Sketching Stories, Stretching Minds*).

The guidance we offer in this chapter comes in two parts: (1) classroom strategies and structures for helping students to write (or express in other media) successfully; and (2) ideas for additional topics related to the various family history activities. Our approach is that a unit such as the family history project provides an excellent opportunity to integrate at least three subject areas—social studies, language arts, and art—thereby saving valuable classroom time. The teacher can achieve much of the teaching of writing skills while covering social studies content and making it especially meaningful. Students' involvement in family history becomes an occasion for giving focused mini-lessons on writing and providing plenty of writing practice, because it's writing the kids are excited about doing and want to do well. Art can create engagement with the material and communicate ideas in powerful ways, as well as help students deepen their written expression. At various points in this book, we offer suggestions for integration with other subjects, particularly social studies and math.

## A KEY STRATEGY: THE CLASSROOM WORKSHOP

Setting up a writing workshop as part of the everyday classroom experience is the ideal way to integrate the craft of writing into the exploration of family history. Fortunately, this structure has been highly developed by many teachers and teacher-authors across the country (see especially Donald Graves, *A Fresh Look at Writing*; Lucy Calkins, *The Art of Teaching Writing*; Nancie Atwell, *In the Middle: New Understandings About Writing, Reading and Learning*; Steven Zemelman and Harvey Daniels, *A Community of Writers*; and Harvey Daniels and Marilyn Bizar, *Methods that Matter*). We can summarize some of their best guidance to help you organize a classroom structure in which you can deliver the most efficient help to students, while maximizing their involvement in writing and their opportunities to get it done. Let's make clear what we mean by "writing workshop."

### Time

Writing workshop involves regularly scheduled blocks of in-class time for students to write, at least thirty minutes at a stretch and at least several times per week. This ensures focus and continuity. It also means scheduling a few minutes for a teacher-guided mini-lesson before kids start writing, and then sharing time—a few minutes for students to hear and respond to each other's writing at the end of the period. Workshop also creates precious time when the teacher can help individual students with particular skills and learning needs.

### Choice

As much as possible, students should have choices of what to work on, how long the piece should be, and other features of the work. No automatic formula exists for how to put a good essay together when it comes to writing up an interview of a partner or describing the cultural history of a family, so students will need to envision options and choose meaningfully among them. Of course, apprentice writers need help learning how to make meaningful choices, and the teacher must provide this through mini-lessons and conferences (see below). But the nature of real writing is centered on making choices—where to focus a piece, which details to include, deciding how to make an idea vivid and understandable. Kids need practice making choices and seeing the outcomes in the work.

### Mini-Lessons

When all or most students in a class need help with a particular skill or strategy, it's efficient for the teacher to conduct a short whole-class lesson on the topic. It is also best to cover a given skill at a point when student writing is likely to incorporate it promptly, so kids get immediate practice with it. A good mini-lesson to help students handle choice, for example, could center on the class brainstorming together some of the options before them. Another example: the pair interview write-up will need focus to keep it from becoming just a bland laundry list about the other person's cultural background. What might that focus be? Some possibilities are:

◆ my partner's family's holiday celebrations;
◆ the history of how my partner's family came to the United States or to our city;

- ◆ foods or clothing or customs that the rest of us don't know much about;
- ◆ a particular relative, such as an uncle or grandmother, whose exploits or experiences help define the family's character;
- ◆ an attitude or value that the family shares.

Students can create their own such list and then, with a volunteer writer, talk through the process of choosing, to see how the thinking might go. Such a lesson will help students write more meaningful essays for the project.

### Conferences

One great advantage of classroom workshop is that it frees the teacher to meet with individual students. Even a very brief, one-to-one lesson is likely to be remembered and applied, and can focus on just what the individual student needs and is ready to learn. And it avoids the whole-class lessons that waste the time of students who've already mastered the skill.

In a half-hour workshop period, you can't get to every student. But a quick *status-of-the-class* survey just before work time will tell you who most needs help and who is ready to work productively on his or her own. Go around the room and have each student state in a phrase what he or she will be working on today. Jot the responses in shorthand on a pad of paper, and you'll have a handy inventory of how the class is progressing.

Short conferences are a highly developed teaching art. You can't solve every problem in the writing at once, and you want the student to do as much of the work as possible; otherwise the writing will reflect your thinking and skills, rather than the student's. One way to solve these challenges is to open the conference by asking several key questions, rather than trying to read and respond immediately to the student's work. Following are three good questions recommended by Donald Graves that can guide your response:

1. What is your piece about?
2. What stage of the work are you at?
3. What help do you want from me?

Once an issue has surfaced, ask the student to do the thinking: "So what can you do about this problem?" If it involves a content revision (rather than just a grammar edit), help the student list two or three options, and ask her to choose which she thinks is best. It's hard to keep from just giving advice, but students will learn more this way and will know the writing is their own.

### Classroom Management

To make workshop run well, you'll need some clear expectations about behavior and the use of work time. The class can draw them up together during a mini-lesson. Keep them positive. You may want a rule about keeping voices low when student pairs are interviewing or holding conferences with each other, one about how to sign up for a conference with the teacher, one about ways to be productive while waiting for a conference with you, and one about things a student can do when finished with a draft. Here are some examples for that last item: review other writings in his or her folder; start a new piece for extra credit; check the draft with his or her partner for accuracy of facts, or with another student to make sure explanations are clear and questions are answered. Put the rules up on a poster so you can easily refer to them when students need a reminder.

## what we got—reality checks
### HOW A CONFERENCE COMBINED WITH SHARING AND A MINI-LESSON TO HELP ONE STUDENT IMPROVE

One day in the course of Steve's visits to Sharon West's third-grade class at Hurley School in Chicago, he knelt next to Beatrice, who had asked him to look at her interview of Baraah. Beatrice, whose family came from Mexico, had included a number of details from Baraah's Palestinian background, including various foods, holidays, and articles of clothing. Steve asked Beatrice what she'd learned about *humus*, the holiday of *Eid*, and the garb called *jillbab*, and Beatrice realized she needed more information from Baraah. Steve also knew Beatrice would need to find a focus for the essay, to give it shape. Sensing that Beatrice was a confident girl, he asked near the end of the period if she'd like to read her piece to the class and get their reactions. After reminding the children to give encouragement as well as to ask questions, Steve and Sharon let the process roll. Not surprisingly, the class asked the same questions Steve had about the various cultural terms. Then as a briefly inserted mini-lesson, he explained to the kids that there probably wouldn't be room in a short essay for all the information, so Beatrice might want to decide how to focus it. Beatrice chose food as her focus, and the period ended. In a follow-up conference the next week, Beatrice showed Steve her revised piece. Now it included a number of Palestinian dishes, but explained just one of them. Steve and Beatrice decided together that a list of terms at the end of the story, with a definition of each—a glossary—would be a good way to explain them (see Beatrice Garza's writing in Chapter 2).

Figures 4.1 and 4.2 show how another student, Luis Garcia, expanded his writing after sharing the first version with the class and fielding their questions.

## A KEY STRATEGY: JOURNALS

Journal-writing time is popular with teachers everywhere. It can be done in a short time at the beginning or end of the day, or just before a transition between activities, putting to good use time that may otherwise be wasted. It gives students the opportunity to write briefly about anything they choose, so it promotes fluency. It doesn't require grading,

Luis Garcia November 24, 1948
Hurley School 302-3
Family history
The things I learned was my great
grandma when she was little she
lived on a farm they raised chickens
and pigs for food. they used a
cast iron stove that burnt wood
for heat and cooking their water was
a well and their bathroom was
built outside. they grew corn to
make tortillas and that was their
bread.

FIGURE 4.1
Luis Garcia's first draft

Who
What
Where
When
Why
how

The thing that was special about the family history project was i learnd that my great grandparents lived on a big farming cent in mexico. It was a long time ago. her name was ?Ruth her family raised chickens and pig's for food. they grew corn to make tortillas and that was their bread. they used a cast iron stove that burnt wood for heating the house and cooking food.
The family had to get water from the well they used it to drink, wash up in, cook with and wash their clothes. they had to go outside to the bathroom it was called a outhouse.

I never new my great grandparents. they Died before i was born. I wish i lived back then on the farm in mexico. I would help them cook and feed the pig's and chickens. I would help them by going to the well to get water. I wish to see what it was like back then on the farm. and to get to know my great grandparents.

**FIGURE 4.2**
Luis Garcia's second draft

though the teacher can periodically and briefly check the journals to see how students are developing and how they're using this tool. How can journals be employed effectively in the family history project?

In a subject area such as this one, where students collect data and then try to make sense of it, the journal is a good place to work on both these key tasks. The journal can be a safe place where students learn to take notes on their interviews with classmates and family members.

Elementary students will often just try to write from memory, and will probably need a mini-lesson on how to jot notes during an interview—a valuable skill for success in later grades. The journal can be a place to list questions before the interview, or follow-up questions after a first effort. And then at the end of a class period of interviewing, or when kids come to class with notes from their home interviews, the teacher can invite students to write in their journal what the interview made them think about, what stands out about the person interviewed, or how they compare that person's experience with their own—to develop perspectives and find themes that give shape to their work.

One key to making journals work is to use them frequently, at the same time each day. We've observed that even in classes with numerous struggling or overactive students, kids who have been writing in journals all year eagerly pull out their notebooks when they see the clock reaching the appointed time—no matter what other activity is taking place.

Here are some ways to enliven journal writing:

### Freewriting

In a mini-lesson, show students how to loosen up by taking a set amount of time—starting with three minutes and building to eight or ten—and writing without pause. If the writer comes to a point where she doesn't know what to say, she writes color words or nonsense words until something comes. This practice often helps blocked writers get started, and surfaces valuable ideas the mind tries to censor or reject as "not good enough."

### Clustering

Students can use charts and diagrams, key words connected by spokes, and chains of associated words to help brainstorm and organize their thoughts. Since writing is limited to a linear, one-dimensional stream of language, two-dimensional graphics help students realize multiple options and connections between ideas. Again, a mini-lesson in which you demonstrate how to create a cluster, brainstorming ideas on a topic with the whole class and arranging them in a web, will help kids see how to do the same thing for themselves. As with any of these strategies, however, it's important to see them as useful aids, not required exercises. Steve discovered, for example, that Beatrice Garza, the most prolific and well-organized writer in Sharon West's third grade, made her webs *after* writing, and only because the teacher required them. For Beatrice, it's all in her head before the web ever comes into existence.

### Dialog Journals

Kids love to pass notes, and this simply legitimizes the desire, putting it to work on your curriculum. Students pair up and after writing an initial short journal entry, swap journals to respond to each other's entries. The idea is not to evaluate the other person's product, but to hold a conversation on paper. The receiving student reads the partner's entry and then responds on the same piece of paper, asking a follow-up question, sharing a similar experience, or extending the writer's thinking, just as one would do in a conversation. Partners swap back and forth several times to get the conversation really moving. And since both partners write simultaneously, it's actually like holding two conversations at once. Be sure the kids understand this so both continue writing steadily, rather than one sitting and watching while the other writes.

### Organizing the Journal into Sections

It's handy for students to divide their journals into sections, so they can keep all their entries on one idea or topic together. That way, as ideas add up, students can review them for expansion into more formal essays. If the kids are using spiral notebooks, have them block off a handful of pages for each topic. Then schedule brief journal-writing times just as a particular lesson or activity is ending, so that students can record their thoughts and reflections on the work they've been doing and where they will be headed next. For the family history project, topics might include:

> notes on family members;
> memories of holiday celebrations;
> notes on partner interview;
> reactions to history events studied;
> reflection—reactions to class activities, thoughts about what it all
>     means;
> questions I have about my family's history, with space for answers.

Be sure to encourage students to look back over their journals whenever they're starting a new essay or inquiry activity, or when they're unsure where to go next on a particular piece of writing, to look for ideas they may have stored away and forgotten.

## A KEY STRATEGY: SKETCH TO STRETCH

Thinking is not always linear. And it's not always in words. Visual art, music, drama, and dance are all powerful ways for students—or for anyone—to gain deeper understanding of an idea. At best, many of us have thought of the arts as a kind of "enrichment"—important for the development of a cultured life and a means of personal expression, but not at the core of the curriculum. What we haven't always understood is that art can serve as a key tool for comprehending traditional written texts, and that it can also stand on its own as one of the most effective ways for students to express and demonstrate thinking and learning. Students who have not been strong in reading or writing often have abilities in other areas such as drawing, drama, and music, strengths that can be developed on their own and be used as bridges to more traditional school modes. However, it's important to know that the teacher does not need to be expert in an art medium to make it work powerfully in the classroom. So we offer one simple and effective artistic structure for student expression here: "sketch to stretch."

The procedure is deceptively simple, yet the more time and close attention you invest, the more you and your students will gain from it. After reading a chapter of a history-related story or textbook, or hearing fellow students' essays on their families' struggles migrating to the United States, students take a few minutes to sketch something that portrays their thoughts and reactions. Then in pairs or small groups, the students take turns explaining their sketches to each another. Finally, a few may share theirs with the whole class.

It's essential that you demonstrate for your students in a mini-lesson that these sketches need not be realistic. Help kids practice using diagrams and geometric shapes. They can picture a favorite character, but they can just as readily portray a feeling, a conflict, a contradiction, or an idea, once they've practiced doing it a few times. High school teachers may find it challenging to teach "symbolism" when kids are studying novels or poetry, but students of all ages quickly and naturally grasp the power of using symbols to illustrate their thoughts about a topic—which is part of what makes the strategy so effective.

The second essential element of sketch-to-stretch is *talk*. The sketches become occasions for students to articulate their thoughts in words as well, and as students explain and comment on their drawings, they often develop additional ideas and understandings. So be sure to allow time for students to explain and discuss their sketches in small groups while you walk around and listen in on as many as possible. As you monitor the discussions, you will be surprised how much you learn about students' comprehension of what they are reading and hearing.

Many teachers learned this strategy from Kathy Short, Jerome Harste, and Carolyn Burke in *Creating Classrooms for Authors and Inquirers*. More recently, Phyllis Whitin, in *Sketching Stories, Stretching Minds*, has shown us through vivid accounts of her own classroom just how much thinking the strategy brings to life.

## reality check

Sharon West helped her third graders at Hurley School to get comfortable with symbolic expression about family history by asking them to create family shields and then to write brief explanations of what they meant. Several of the shields with their explanations are shown in Figures 4.3–4.6.

## further topics for exploring family history

Outlined below are a number of topics for student writing and/or artistic expression that can deepen and enrich the family history project. These may be initiated at any point during the project at which the teacher observes that students are ready to delve more fully into the material they've been gathering, or realizes they need a structured step to help deepen their engagement. They can certainly be employed as whole-class assignments, but their most effective use will be in student-centered workshop-style classrooms, where they serve as enticing options and alternatives from which students may choose, based on what they are discovering about their own families.

### 1. HEROES AND SHEROES—PICK ONE

As your students get into their stride filling out classroom profiles, kinship charts, and time lines, and as they start bringing in documents and photos, they will need to find ways to tell the stories of their families as narratives. Focusing on one person and considering what makes him or her important to the family is one way to make these stories come alive.

Ask your students to spend time thinking about and choosing one ancestor or living relative to write about. They may need journal-writing time to work their memories and jot details about each of a few favorite relatives before choosing one. If you see that your students are having difficulty connecting with specifics, guide them through a memory

**FIGURE 4.3**
Manal Gouleh's family shield. "The flag stands for where I came from. The sword stands for bad times in my country. The arrow stands for love. The hawk stands for Hurley Hawks. The colors stand for my favorite colors."

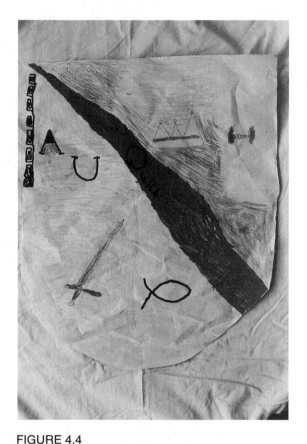

**FIGURE 4.4**
Daniel Quick's family shield. "The Greek key stands for Greece. The A and Ω the mean beginning to end in the Greek alphabet. My family sticks together. The crown stands for God. The weights stand for strength. The sword means fight through bad times. The fish stands for the Christians. The heart is for love. The arms are for friendship. The crown with the cross means loyalty."

search similar to the following. For each person they're considering, students jot down, if they can recall it:

- a time they can remember when they were with this person (if his or her life span has overlapped with theirs);
- some accomplishment or special action or event that the person experienced;

FIGURE 4.5

Jose Chavez's family shield. "I drew a sword. It stands for bravery. The colors I chose were red for bravery and blue for loyalty. I drew a tree that was green. The color green stands for youth, strength and hope nature. I drew rocks. They were silver. I chose silver because of peace. I drew a crown. It was gold. I chose gold because it is valor, joy and honor. I also drew a baseball bat it was gold also."

FIGURE 4.6

Miguel Aguilera's family shield. "The cross means we believe in Jesus. The Angel means my middle name. The axes mean to be strong. I drew the wolf because it is my favorite animal. The color blue means I go to Catholic school also. The color yellow means peace. The color black because that is my favorite color. I colored white for the wind."

◆ a habit or aspect of personality the person was known for;
◆ something the person said that seemed important, or that stands out in the student's memory;
◆ things other people in the family say about this person.

Students may not have memories or knowledge in every one of these categories for every person on their list, but if they find information piling up around one particular person, they know they've found a hot prospect, someone they have a connection with and know enough about to create an in-depth portrait. Once students have made their choice, ask them to gather all the materials and references they have uncovered about that person, such as photos, interview notes, journal entries describing their own memories, obituaries, and birth certificates.

After this material has been assembled, the students will be ready for a more in-depth memory search and organizing brainstorm. Clustering is a good strategy for this work. Students can write the person's name in the middle of a piece of paper and begin constructing a web of ideas and remembrances around it. Help your students to relax and loosen up their creative powers as they work on this web. Ask the class questions as they immerse themselves in the story:

Have you known this person personally?
What do you remember most about this person?
What are some distinctive features of this person's personality?
Can you remember actual things this person said?
What did this person's voice sound like?
What did this person look like—hair, eyes?
Do you remember specific incidents about the person that reveal what he or she was like?
What are some typical things this person might have done on an ordinary day?
When was this person born? How?
Where? What was that place like?
What was happening in the big world during this person's lifetime?
How might those events have affected this person's decisions and choices?

Help your students jot down phrases and leads, ideas to pursue. If they have a photograph, what does it suggest about this person and time? If students lack answers to some of the questions, whom might they ask to fill in a detail or give another perspective on the life and personality of this person?

Don't try to do any more than this in one session. Just build the web. Set up some ideas to pursue. At the end, each student should have a paper covered with phrases related to the person in question. This is deep reflective time, time to pursue questions, to allow ideas to emerge and take form. Give your students a few days to follow up their questions, make calls, and talk to relatives. Help them to choose and focus on one or two key incidents or aspects of the person's life that best help us understand what makes the person special and shows us what he or she is (was) like. Then it's time to write, using a classroom workshop.

## reality checks

Tank Elementary School in Green Bay, Wisconsin, is a warm and welcoming school with a population that includes a large number of Hmong children. Multiage fourth/fifth-grade teachers Mary Tomasiak and Dan Jones invited the children in their class to write up family stories and portraits, illustrate them, and put them together in a Family History Project book. The following, Mai Lor Vang's contribution, is not a descriptive portrait, but outlines a harrowing journey of escape that makes it clear why her father is a hero. Her illustration is seen in Figure 4.7.

### My Family History
#### by Mai Lor Vang

Hi! My name is Mai Lor Vang. I'm 11 years old and I'm in fourth grade. My name Mai Lor means daughter of the Lor clan. I was born in Laos. I have two sisters and five brothers. I live with my mother. I like to play jump rope, basketball, and soccer. I like vegetables. My friends are Mai Soua, Sia Mee, Pa Yang, and Mai Doua. I like school. There are nine people in my family. I have five brothers. Their names are Hue, Long, Sen Sai, Soua Sao, and Zong. I have two sisters—Mai Moua and Mai Blia. My mom and my cousin moved because the Vietnamese came after us and tried to kill my dad, but he ran away. My dad told my mom we were going to hide. Then my grandpa and my grandma came to help my dad. My dad and my grandpa said everybody hiding in the jungle did not have enough food. They were hungry. My grandpa and my dad decided that we should go away to Thailand. On the way to Thailand everyone was hungry and there was not enough milk for the babies. My dad led the way to Thailand. When we got to Thailand, we had food to eat and everyone was happy. The Americans asked if we like to go to America. We said yes. Then we went there and we were so happy. In America my mom's sisters came and picked us up. We lived with my mom's sister. Then my dad came to take us to Green Bay. We have lived in Green Bay two years. The Americans in Green Bay give money to my family. Now my mom and dad have a job.

Illustrated by _Mai Lor Vang_

FIGURE 4.7
Mai Lor Vang's hero—her father

One way to help students focus is to pose the assignment a bit differently, as in the following example, based on the students' reading about the author of the book *Family Pictures*:

## Family History

*Carmen Lomas Garza was inspired by her mother to become an artist. Her mother always told her to dream of her future and follow that dream.*

*Think about a family member that has inspired you and write about that member. How did they inspire you and what did they inspire you to do?*

My Aunt Alica works very hard. She went to Bradley University for 4 years, she has a degree in engineering. She is only 25 years old and my aunt help to design the 1999 Cadillac. My aunt lives in Southfield, Michigan, but in December she will be in Janesville, Wisconsin at the General Motors plant to help design a new car. When I grow up I will go to college just like her but I will be a lawyer and my aunt will be there to help me. End of story.

Chanelle

## 2. HEROES AND SHEROES—ZOOM IN ON THEIR LIFE

A life is a huge thing. People are complicated marvels. When good writing sounds real, the reader recognizes something authentic in it. It makes the person who's being described come alive. This requires attention to detail, zooming in on small things. Teachers talk a lot about adding detail to writing, but we need to do more than just exhort students. We must illustrate for them just how important detail is, help them take the time to gather and surround themselves with information and artifacts about their subject, and then select a few pieces to focus on. It's especially important to help students find a focus, one particular group or arrangement of details that make sense of the family hero or she-ro. A laundry list of scattered details can easily fill up the page, but it doesn't necessarily help us appreciate the person.

### Demonstrating the Power of Focus and Detail

Prepare sheets of black construction paper by cutting out a one-by-two-inch rectangle in the middle of each sheet. Give one sheet to each student and ask the students to hold up their sheet and look around the room. Ask them to notice what happens as they move the sheet closer and farther from their eyes. Have them try holding the sheet at arm's length, capturing small pieces of the room in the frame. Let them take some time to look at small parts of things, patterns, and blocks of color.

Have them sketch some of these "views" in their journals or on blank paper. Afterward, talk together about what happens to their awareness of things in the room as a result of this exercise. In writing, we can achieve the same sort of awareness and intensification that the frame helps us achieve for seeing.

On an overhead projector, share an example of detailed writing about a person—using either your own writing, an excerpt from a piece of good literature, or a good student sample—and help students see the connection between your visual experiment and the good writing that brings a portrait to life. Now, have your students once again gather the information they have on their subject, including the web sheet. Does anything else need to be added? Updated?

Next, students should take the black framing sheet and slide it over their assembled materials—over the faces in photographs, the dates on death certificates, the entry in a Bible, the old letter. Place it on the web. Look at the different entries. What do they evoke? Students can decide, once again, which one they'd like to begin writing about, deepening into a portrait of this relative or ancestor.

When students have made a decision, have them start a new web on this subject. Or if they appear ready, take ten minutes to freewrite. Donald Graves says, Put your pen on the paper and keep it moving for ten minutes. At the end of this or the next writing workshop period, have several student volunteers share what they've written. In the following example, the student chose to focus on the grandfather's job as a police sergeant.

> While working on my family history project I was interested in my grandpa because he said he was a sergeant at his job being a police. His name is Isaac Ellis. He became a sergeant in 1996. September 5, 1996. In the city of Chicago. His job was to help the city be safer. He went to some schools and told the students how to be safe in the city. He said never do drugs. And he said to never talk to strangers and never take a treat from a stranger. He said to me to never forget this.
>
> I am proud that he is my grandpa because he always sticks up for me. He protects me from bullies and gang members that try to kill neighbors. I'm also proud of him because he does not let the community down. He retired in 1998 but he still watches out for people in the community. He does not want people to destroy our neighborhood.
>
> Izel Ellis

If regular workshop time is devoted to writing, a whole portfolio of portraits can be created, with various ones at different stages of completion. The teacher can require a certain number of finished works within a given time frame. But regular writing practice on subjects of the students' choice will improve writing over time.

## 3. LETTER WRITING

Letter writing has always been practiced in schools, but in the family history project, it becomes real. When a student has reached a dead end in the search for information, he or she may need to write to a relative, county recorder, newspaper, author, or historian for specific information. It's good to help students do the job effectively.

Have materials available to send letters—stationery, envelopes, and stamps. Students may have to research to find addresses and zip codes. They'll need help learning the customary format for composing a business letter. You can give a mini-lesson on letter writing, as part of a writer's workshop, with examples on the overhead and posters on the wall that students can refer to as they work. Be sure to include examples of both formal business letters to governmental agencies and more personal letters directed to family members.

Students may also need help tuning in to the needs of their audience. Why does the writer want this information? What exactly is he or she asking for? This is a good occasion to learn about clarity, since it will have clear consequences. Kids can serve as good peer editors for one another in this situation, for anything one's partner doesn't understand is likely to be misunderstood by a clerk in an office somewhere as well. Place students in pairs and instruct one to role play—to pretend to be the census clerk or the favorite uncle—while the other reads his or her draft letter. The listener should ask any questions he or she needs answered to fully understand and respond to the inquiry. The writer should take notes and plan to add the further explanations to the letter. Then have them switch roles so that both members of the pair get help.

Your students will experience the frustration of seeking information from governmental bureaucracies and the emotional high of making first contact with a distant relative. Figure 4.8 shows Christina Winfrey's letter to Oprah Winfrey, which was discussed in the Introduction. These communications with vastly different audiences can, with luck, deliver great surprises and rewards over time. Letters sent and received become historians' primary source materials.

February 28, 1996

Mrs. Oprah Winfrey
Harpo Studios
Chicago, IL.

Dear Ms. Winfrey
    My name is Christina Winfrey. I am a fifth grader at McDowell Elementary School. Since October I've been researching my ancestors and relatives. With the help of my family, Mrs. Murray, (my teacher) and Mrs. Bearden from the Family History Project, I have learned a lot.
    One of the most exciting things I've learned is that my grandfather's father, Nathaniel Winfrey, and your father, Vernon Winfrey, are brothers! So that makes us cousins.
    I asked my grandfather James Winfrey, if I'm related to you. He told me about the family Bible. In it are the names of my ancestors and relatives.
    So there's my proof cousin Oprah! Now maybe we could get together and you could take my class on a tour of your studio. I would you like to take a picture with you and we could compare our kinship charts.

Please write or call

Love,
Christina

FIGURE 4.8
Letter from Christina Winfrey to Oprah Winfrey (information about the relationship was slightly incorrect and was corrected in a second letter)

## 4. INTERVIEWS

Interviewing produces firsthand information from living sources of knowledge. We often urge our students to interview their oldest living relative, but every relative is a worthy subject for insights into family history. This important genre of writing requires skills that can be fully developed only by extensive practice.

We've already described in an earlier chapter how to help students through role playing and practice in class. We can also provide them with examples of well-done interviews, help on producing good questions to ask, and practice in various methods of recording testimony (note taking, audio- and videotaping). We should help them remember that they need to be respectful of and attentive to the people they interview. The person they interview may need to schedule a time to talk; may feel it is silly to be formally interviewed by someone closely related; may need to take breaks and be allowed time to remember.

A number of relatives could be interviewed over the course of a family history project, but have your students start by selecting one. Perhaps the greatest challenge for student interviewers is to identify a topic about which the interviewee has some knowledge and involvement, as opposed to inquiring about something only the interviewer considers important. The questioner must start with broad, open-ended questions to give the person a chance to indicate what he or she has to share. We must help our students learn how to listen for signs and hints that a significant topic is being uncovered as the interviewee responds—gestures, tones of voice, beginnings of longer stories, and phrases such as, "That reminds me of the time when. . . ." Learning how to focus with more specific follow-up questions once a productive topic is identified is also an art.

One way to do this with a grandfather, for example, is to inquire about his life in connection to a period in U.S. history he's lived through, say, the 1940s. The student can ask questions about a broad range of social, economic, cultural, and technological influences that affected his life during this period. Provide students with a chart of key events from the period, and go over them together in a brief history lesson. Your chart might look like this:

## 1940s American History

Tell me things you remember about . . .
- World War II—America fighting Germany in Europe;
- World War II—America fighting Japan in the Pacific;

- the war effort in the United States—women working in weapons factories;
- the first atomic bomb;
- helping damaged countries recover after the war;
- the cold war with Russia;
- the GI Bill, which helped returning soldiers after the war.

## Other Aspects of Life

Tell me things you remember about . . .
- entertainment—music at that time; radio programs; movies; the first TV sets;
- sports—famous teams; great players;
- work—what jobs were like; how bosses treated you; unions;
- home—cooking; what helpful appliances you had or didn't have; what your house was like;
- surroundings—where you lived; what it looked like; what special places were there;
- customs—how people dressed; how they talked; what they did to socialize;
- problems—the things people worried about; discrimination; people who were excluded from jobs, neighborhoods, and so on.

It's important to help students realize, however, that no chart or guide can do the thinking for them. In fact, if it leads to just a long list of short answers, it becomes more of a hindrance than a help. Interviewers must listen closely and try to tell when a particular topic is of special interest to the person they are interviewing, then zero in with follow-up questions. Ethnographers, who study the characteristics of various cultures, have developed guides for asking questions to learn as much as possible about an aspect of someone's life from that person's point of view. A productive approach is to encourage the person to list various things he or she can remember about a particular event or aspect of life, rather than mentioning just one. Students who learn how to gather data this way are learning a complex and important analytical skill.

The following are examples of good follow-up questions:

- Tell me more about . . .
- Tell me all the various things you can remember about . . .
- Where did this take place? Tell me all the things you can remember about what it was like there.
- When was it? How old were you?

- So what happened next? What were some of the causes of . . . What were some of the results of . . .
- How did you go about doing that?
- Who else was involved? What did they have to do with it?
- Why did that happen? What were some reasons why . . .
- What were some of your feelings about it?

Students will need help understanding that although they will probably obtain a great deal of information, they will very likely not include all of it when they write up their interview. Telling one in-depth story about one aspect or event in someone's life will help us picture him or her much more vividly than a long list of disconnected details. If you read aloud to children examples of focused and unfocused portraits, for a mini-lesson, you will find that the students immediately recognize which is more effective.

Interviews are a researcher's dream. They give testimony and color to history. When your students interact with relatives, they honor their life and experience. They practice the skillful art of asking good questions and waiting for good answers. They take notes and synthesize ideas. And they learn to relate personal experiences to public history.

## reality check

As students gain practice, they are able to develop more focus and detail. High school student Maira Rodriguez's piece takes her cousin's information and stories about growing up in Mexico and turns all of it into a narrative in the cousin's voice:

"Samira it's time to get up to go to school," mom always said. Now I don't know what I'd do if our roosters ever stopped waking up at dawn. Must hurry to catch the "panadera" (lady who sold freshly made bread) before she leaves or else we won't have breakfast again today. I got the table set with fresh milk, bread, and some coffee. "Marcos, Javier get up guys." "Oh! Do we have to, five more minutes, come on please." No! The water's also ready for you so hurry up before the water and your breakfast get cold. We're all eating quite quickly so we could get to school on time.

School is half an hour away from here so we walk. It's a real pain because I have to listen to my younger brother complain all the time, but eventually we get there. My best friend is always there before I am, at the end of school she always accompanies us home.

If it wasn't for her I'd be home alone with my two younger brothers. I'd hurry up and get everything ready for dinner. In the mean while I'd sweep the whole house, feed all our animals and wash some clothes. Sometimes I'd be so busy that I would forget to do my school work. One day went by real quick over there. Of course next day I'd get punished for that. I'd always have to watch my younger brothers, because since my parents were always working nobody else could watch them, so I did. Our little farm depended on their work. My parents practically killed themselves working for the wealthier families. They'd go from 5:00 A.M. til whatever time they were done picking the Jamaica (plant to make a type of cool aid) and most of the time it was 6:00 or 7:00 P.M. I was only 10 years old when I had all those responsibilities. I always felt I didn't enjoy my childhood. Especially since my older sister left us when she was real young to get married and move. . . .

## 5. TIME LINE VIGNETTES

When they construct their Life Time Line (see Chapter 6), your students will first concentrate on its form and order. Then they'll have to decide on the most important events and set them correctly on the line with dots, hash marks, or arrows. Each of these moments has a story embedded in it—a deep and complex story. As teachers, we can help our students bring that story out in short pieces of writing. Compiled, these stories become autobiographies.

Have your students look at some of the events on their time lines more closely. If you introduced the framing sheet described in Activity 2—the black construction paper with a small rectangle cut out of the center—you can ask students to get it out and run it over the time line, focusing on and thinking about one event at a time. Help them think about and select a particular event and do some prewriting activity around it—at first just to see if there's enough material there to expand into a longer written piece.

When writing about oneself, visualization is an especially valuable tool for retrieving important detail. You can guide students through this by asking them to put down their pencils, relax, and focus on the specific event they've chosen. Talk them through the process *very* slowly, so they can observe every detail in their mind's eye. Silently count slowly to five between phrases, to allow students to think and search their memories. Here's one way to provide this guidance:

*Let yourself return to the place and the time that this important event happened. . . . Now take a good look around you . . . and notice things you see to your right . . . and to your left . . . the objects . . . and what the place looks like. . . . Notice whether other people are there, and if so, what they are doing . . . and what they are saying . . . Other sounds you hear . . . and what is happening . . . and what you feel about it. And now you can let the event happen, only this time you are watching it, like a movie before your eyes . . .*

When the visualization is over, students can quickly jot down the details they will probably now remember. Most will be ready to write, with plenty to tell. And along with their own personal stories, they will, through the course of the project, gather stories about other family members. Ultimately, if students write about numerous events, the pieces can be mounted on the time line itself or published as a small booklet. Elaborating on these moments will help deepen the time line and students' appreciation of their history, provide another reason for writing, and produce a valuable family document. The actual connecting of these autobiographical pieces to the larger span of public history is a further step in the process, described in Chapter 6.

## reality check

Third-grader Amelia Partida chose to focus a vignette not on herself but on her grandfather. Her first draft contained plenty of details, but in no particular order, with reactions to her grandfather's accident coming before the event itself. For a mini-lesson on sequencing, Amelia bravely shared her paper with the class. After we numbered the sentences on the chalkboard, she rearranged them one by one in a new, more chronological order while we watched. Figure 4.9 shows the result.

### 6. DIGGING UP BIRTHDAYS

Being born is an overwhelmingly personal event for parents and children. Yet in the big world, life does go on. Birth dates are set in public history. By looking up old newspapers or magazines from that moment in history, students will get a sense of the issues of the day. They will also get experience using library microfilm archives.

You can start by reading aloud *On the Day You Were Born* by Debra Frasier. Students can then develop a list of questions about what was happening on the day they were born. The research can proceed along two lines: information on local and national events from newspapers and periodicals, and individual memories from parents or grandparents.

For the first line of inquiry, you will need to arrange a trip to a library that has microfilm or hard copies of archived periodicals. The

Amelia Partida                December 14, 1998
Hurly School                  Room 302

    My grandpa was 20 years old. He was working in a Shoe factory the machine got out of control. My grandpa pressed the wrong botton it cut off his tumb and his finger next to his tumb. He had to be rushed to the Hospital he was rushed to Christ hospital. They had Pixed his tumb and this other finger. Then my grandpa called the house then my mom answerd it when my grandpa told her what happend she storied to cry then my grandma was in her room my mom told my grandma what happend to she storied cry also. He weres a glove so nobody can see it. Then we saw a guy and it was my grandpa my grandma was happy. He still can fit things and lift things also.

FIGURE 4.9
Amelia Partida sequences her story about her grandfather

librarian can explain to your students how to request specific news periodicals for specific dates, and procedures for using microfilm machines.

Once students have their chosen document on the screen, they will want to look at headlines, big and small. Anything surprising? Many students will need help with background information about ongoing political or societal events and issues at the time of their birth. Have them jot down at least three items that catch their attention and obtain a photocopy of the page(s) on which the articles appeared. If time allows, have them look up the date that their parents were born and a newspaper from the city of their birth, if available. Make copies for future writing and research.

The next step is for the students to ask a parent or grandparent about memories and stories of the day the child was born. Another good book to read for this, with a Native American perspective, is the dramatic

*Knots on a Counting Rope* by Bill Martin and John Archambault. It's an excellent example of family storytelling between child and grandparent, and a good lesson about overcoming a disability as well. If you have students who are adopted or not living with their parents, you can help them ask their guardians about the first day they came to their current home. Students can use the interviewing techniques described in Activity 4 to guide their information gathering. As a special interview topic, this evocative memory never fails to bring vivid answers. A mother's remembrance of the day of birth is strikingly different from the newspapers' weighing of events. Put side by side, they give added depth to the student's understanding of this important moment.

Your students can now use the information they've gathered to write a short essay about what was happening in the world and in their parents' lives on the day they were born. What surprised them? What were the big stories of the day? Your students may develop this story into a longer essay or leave it for the time being as part of their writer's notebook. Either way, they will have learned valuable research skills, obtained firsthand documentary information about an important moment in their family history, and discovered how that moment was linked to events in the big world. They have practiced writing and added to their portfolio of information on family history.

## reality check

Name: Mindy Campbell
Interview with: Andrea and Mark Campbell, my parents
Date: December 1998
Hebron Middle School
Title: My Birth

My mom said that she had a beautiful baby. My dad said that I was a cutie and that I was funny. I was really mean to other babies when I went to birthday parties and I would always be in trouble. My dad said it was kind of cute how ornery I was.

When I asked my parents about the time I was born they liked talking about it. My mom was more than nine months pregnant with her second child. The doctors had to induce her labor so I would be born but it didn't work. When my mom came home at 11:00 P.M. her water broke. It was November 28, 1985. Then she went into labor. My dad took my mom to the hospital. By then it was around 12:00. My mom was in labor all day but I wouldn't come out. The doctor took my mom's blood pressure and then he took mine. My blood pressure was way down so they rushed my mom into surgery. There they put my mom to sleep and cut her stomach open and took me out. By then it was 8:16 P.M. on November 29, 1985. They sewed my mom's stomach and gave me to my dad. I was 8.5 pounds and 19 inches long. I had red hair and blue eyes. They named me Melinda Nicole Campbell and nicknamed me Mindy. My mom went home two days later on December 1, 1985.

This story is remembered because it was the birth of their second daughter. I still am ornery but not as bad as I used to be. My dad said I was as ornery then as I am now except it was cute when I was little.

Mindy could now check newspaper headlines to see what was happening in the rest of the world that day. Since it was the day after Thanksgiving, it was a quiet news day, at least as far as the local and national news was concerned, but here's what was going on:

- Israel agreed to return secret U.S. documents that were stolen by a spy.
- Rockets were fired at two South African oil refineries by guerrillas fighting apartheid.
- In Guatemala, seven human rights workers investigating people's disappearances were expelled by the government.
- American astronauts on the *Atlantis* satellite were reported eating Thanksgiving turkey and launching the biggest communications satellite ever.
- Alligators were making a comeback in Florida as a result of being listed as an endangered species for the previous eighteen years. Some people wanted to allow alligator hunts, but environmentalists opposed it.
- The Detroit Lions football team beat New York to advance their at-home record to 6–0.

## 7. FAMILY HISTORY QUILTS

Quilting has become an increasingly popular mode for artistic expression in schools, perhaps because it taps into American tradition, and promotes and portrays a sense of community. In 1998, the City of Chicago Department of Cultural Affairs, the Art Institute of Chicago, and the Chicago Arts Partnerships in Education collaborated to build on the growing interest in quilts in the schools. Visiting artists, teachers, parent volunteers, and students in twenty schools planned and created quilts on a variety of themes. Several focused on family history.

For this activity, students must first choose their theme or topic from among the family history investigations they've been pursuing. Then they sketch on paper the design or picture expressing the chosen item in their family's history. Some quilt projects involve painting designs, using fabric paint; some use appliqué with colored fabrics; and some use a combination of the two. Experienced quilters can help you select the appropriate material for creating the quilt, muslin for the squares and backing, batting, colored fabric scraps, quilter's pins, fabric crayons, markers, paints, and so on. You and the students will need to do lots of careful measuring to determine correct widths and lengths for sashing (divider strips between quilt squares), borders, and seams at the edges of each square. Students use their drawings to guide them in creating the actual images out of cloth or paint. If they are using appliqué, they'll need to practice stitching first before sewing fabric pieces onto their quilt square. Some teachers and artists teach students decorative embroidery stitches to embellish parts of their images. Next comes the sewing of quilt squares to the sashing strips and quilt borders. The last steps involve attaching the decorated top layer to the batting and backing. This is the actual "quilting," which means stitching that runs throughout the quilt to hold the layers securely together. This can be done using a sewing machine or by hand quilting. Most quilts also have a binding around the outside to finish off the edges.

Some excellent resources are available on the Internet to help with making quilts. They include:

- Heddi Craft's Quilting with Children: *http://ariel.ccs.brandeis.edu/~heddi/*
- Index-Lisa's Texas Quilting Page Links: *http://home.sprynet.com/sprynet/mrmago01/quilting.htm*
- Math Quilts: *http://members.aol.com/mathquilt/*
- Planet Patchwork: *www.planetpatchwork.com*
- Quilters Coloring Book: *www.geocities.com/Heartland/Acres/6982*
- World Wide quilting Page: *http://quilt.com/Quilt.html*

## reality check

At Mitchell school, teachers Ted Lesley and Margaret Kania guided their fourth-grade bilingual students to create a quilt (see the cover of this book) in which each square tells the story of parents meeting, falling in love, getting married, and having a family. The teachers reported:

One quilt block tells of a boy and girl, each walking their dog in the park; they meet, become friends and eventually marry. Many blocks display their parents' wedding. The students were enthusiastic from beginning to end, from interviewing their parents and writing their stories, to designing and creating their quilt squares, and sharing their stories with others. The project showed the dedication that students are willing to give when they are involved in a project that holds meaning for them. They were proud to see their twenty squares united in a public display dedicated to their families.

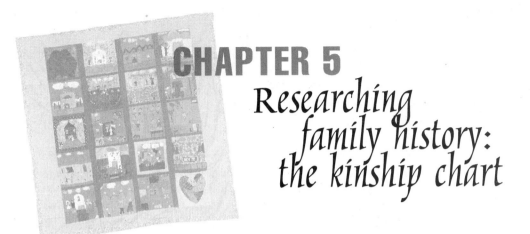

# CHAPTER 5
# Researching
# family history:
# the kinship chart

our students have interviewed each other and one or more of
their parents, guardians, or other family members. They've
charted and compared similarities and differences among their
backgrounds. Perhaps they've also written a portrait of a favorite
family member, or a memory of a particular moment in their own life
in that family. They're hooked and ready for more intense and challenging inquiry into their family's history. Research, instead of being that musty march to create stacks of note cards and fuss over the etiquette of footnote citations, is about to come alive for them, a drama of discovery. There will also be some frustration, since not every piece of information can be readily traced, so we must help students accept it, at least in small doses. Students hope intensely to find that key reference to an ancestor in the census document they are painstakingly searching through. In this stage of the family history project, the students are not *studying* history so much as *doing* what historians do.

In this workshop, students use kinship charts—family trees—to organize their research. The formal kinship chart is a systematic, graphic representation of a direct bloodline back into history. It identifies the names of one's ancestors and relatives, as well as the dates and places of their birth, marriage, and death, from generation to generation. However, as this is one of the most widely used activities in the family history repertoire, teachers have learned that they must be flexible and provide students with a wide set of choices for their research. Children who are adopted or living with foster parents can learn the history of the families they've become part of. They can create nongenealogical trees that include all the adults who are important to them. "Ancestors" can be defined as the parents, grandparents, and great-grandparents of any of the important adults in their lives.

Children whose families immigrated as a result of recent conflicts or political turmoil—Hmong families from Laos, for example, or Bosnian refugees—may find it difficult to obtain much written information on their families' past in their countries of origin, but may wish simply to learn more about the world they left behind. They may want to understand the conditions that led their families to leave and come here. Or they may desire to learn more of the culture their parents hope to preserve. Joyce Maguire Pavao of the Center for Family Connections and Pre/Post Adoption Consulting Team in Cambridge, Massachusetts, says, "It's a much more complicated assignment than people think for African-American children, relatives of victims of the Holocaust or some child who spent his or her first ten years in a Romanian orphanage" (*New York Times*, Feb. 7, 1999, pp. 1, 51). So although we will focus in this chapter on gathering data from genealogical records and Internet Web sites (since these are technical resources not every teacher is familiar with), teachers should plan alternatives for those students who cannot obtain much information from those sources.

Digging for this information teaches valuable skills in using both primary and secondary sources—that is, people who can describe their own experience, and the books and documents that record events. Scouring archives and family materials requires attention to detail. It takes tenacity, creativity, and time. Interviewing relatives requires tact, patience, and the ability to listen. Research using documents is, of course, the more traditional kind done in school. Yet some of our best research sources live with us or are available by phone or mail. The dialogue begun by a student's inquiry into his or her history strengthens the family. It is infectious and produces treasured portfolios that can be passed on and added to, as part of a family's heritage.

Kinship charts come in many forms. We've included the more traditional type in Figure 5.1. It lays out as a backward-branching tree—the child's two parents, four grandparents, eight great-grandparents, their parents, and so on. It can be valuable, however, to work the other way, starting with a great- or great-great-grandparent and working forward as in Figure 5.2, listing siblings, aunts and uncles, and so on—particularly if a student discovers she has a famous living relation and wants to discover how they are linked. Be sure to include a nongenealogical tree with unlabeled branches as an alternative, as in Figure 5.3. Or create your own hybrid. Students from families that have recently (i.e., in the past several generations) immigrated to this country may need to depend more on the Internet, rather than the census and other documents

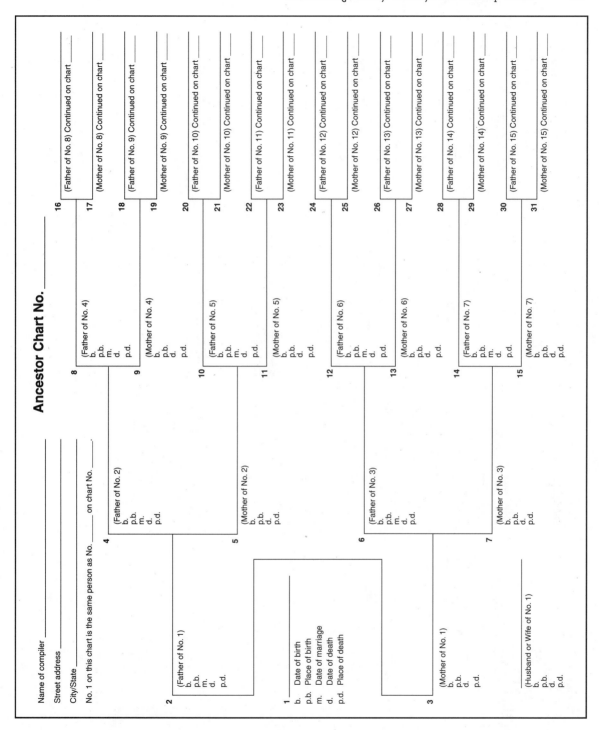

**FIGURE 5.1**

Traditional kinship chart (from: Eugene Provenzo, Jr., Asterie Baker Provenzo, and Peter A. Zorn, Jr. 1984. *Pursuing the Past: Teacher's Guide,* p. 71. Reading, MA: Addison-Wesley)

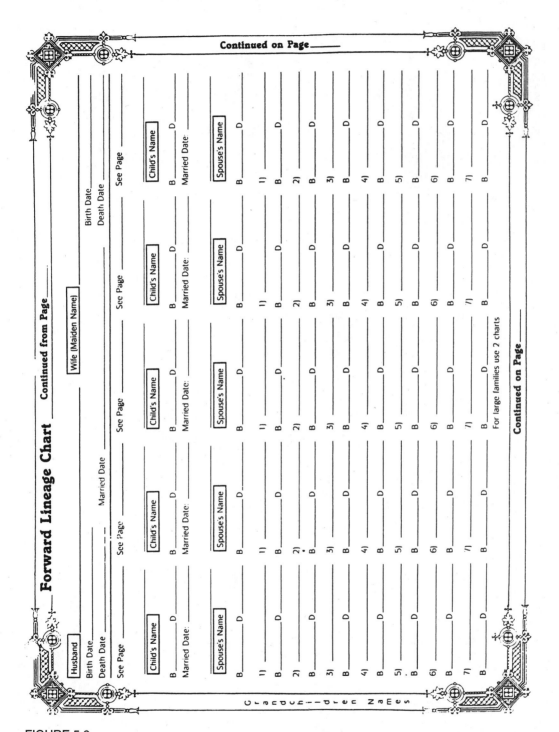

FIGURE 5.2

Kinship chart that works forward from common ancestor (from George Allerton. 1991. *Do It Yourself Family History: Our Family History and Records.* Orfield, PA: Associated Specialties)

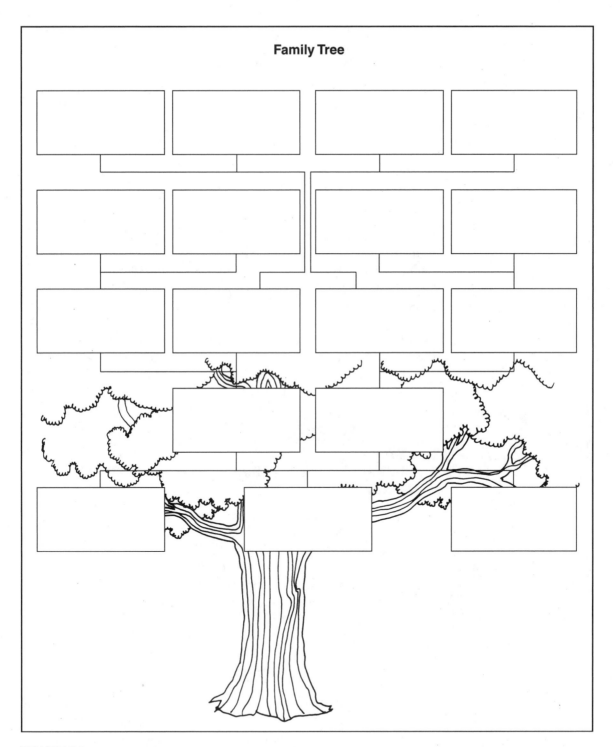

FIGURE 5.3
Nonstructured family tree

available for families long in the United States, but it's surprising just how much information is available, waiting to be uncovered.

The best way to prepare to conduct this activity is to try it yourself, before you start with your class. As you do the work, you will quickly realize what stumbling blocks you'll need to help the kids through, and what pleasures hide in making new discoveries. Start with a blank kinship chart, begin with yourself, and fill in as many slots as possible. Whatever you don't know, skip over. Those blank spaces will then lead your inquiry into your family's past. Find all the documents you can. If your parents or grandparents live in another city, make a few phone calls, ask them for all the facts, names, and dates they know, and see if they'll find and fax or mail you copies of documents they have. Birth, death, marriage, citizenship, and immigration papers all contain a wealth of information. They often name the parents of the person on the document, leading you back another generation. Collect the oldest family photos you can find. If you live near a genealogical archive, try to obtain census documents on your family (see the list of National Archives branches in Step 4). Try the Internet yourself, using the Web site list in Step 4. And most important, talk to the oldest family member available to you. He or she is your treasure. Take good notes or tape record your conversation. Along with names and dates, leave time for stories to unfold.

## how-to guide
### STEP 1:
### CONDUCT A MINI-LESSON SHARING YOUR OWN KINSHIP CHART

When you're satisfied that you have a good start on your own research, make overhead copies of your kinship chart and some of the documents and pictures you've unearthed. Your search, your experience, will be the model for your students as they begin. Share these artifacts and research processes with your students to help turn them on to this next family history task, to show how the task is done, and to illustrate what the results might look like.

### STEP 2:
### FILLING IN WHAT THEY KNOW

After describing your own family's journey, take your students step by step through the kinship chart as shown in Figure 5.1. The traditional form of the chart begins with the student inquirer, No. 1, filling in date of birth, place of birth, and so on. No. 2 is the student's father. Many students will have heard and can remember some of the information. Students should just fill in what they know at this point. But help the kids to add additional information that may not be asked for on the chart. Was the father born here? Yes? No? Why did he move here?

Next move on to No. 3, the student's mother. In standard genealogical charts, the even numbers are always males, and the odd numbers females. Standard charts are concerned only with bloodlines—fathers, mothers, grandfathers and grandmothers, and so on, not brothers, cousins, or uncles. If you're using a hybrid chart, be sure to help the kids understand its logic.

Continue on through the chart, giving students time to remember and ask questions. When most have finished, ask for comments on how things went. Are they more surprised by what they know, or by what they don't know?

## STEP 3:
## CONSULTING FAMILY MEMBERS

For homework, the students take their charts home and start gently prodding parents and guardians for information. Relatives can be called and recalled for promised information. Help your students become aware of the many documents and items that can yield data. Parents and guardians can search for birth certificates and marriage certificates stashed away in drawers and file cabinets. Old photographs with approximate dates and accompanying texts can be collected. In some families, dates of relatives' births and/or deaths are recorded in family Bibles, so these should be consulted. Students can be given large envelopes to carry documents in. It's wise to make photocopies and return the original documents home. All new information gathered from these sources should be entered onto the genealogical chart.

Usually, when students return for the next class, some are itching to show off the gold they've uncovered. But before the sharing begins, have your students write in their journals about how the inquiry process went for them. By allowing time and space for this reflection, students who received an early setback will have an honored place to share even that experience, and you'll learn who needs extra help or encouragement to find another avenue of inquiry. A *status of the class* report, with brief oral statements from each student, will help reveal the same kinds of ongoing assessment information. Usually within a few days, the competition to bring in documents and stories accelerates, so if your time is limited sharing has to be kept to one or two treasured artifacts.

## STEP 4:
## DIGGING INTO THE ARCHIVES

It's surprising just how easy it is to gain access to archival records such as census files, birth and death certificates, school records, deeds, wills, and obituaries. At the end of this book is a list of addresses for individual state archives. For students whose families have lived in the United States since the nineteenth or early twentieth century, these can yield information that allows them to piece together more and more of their family's history. Students in the earliest grades will not yet have the skills or patience for this step—though we've seen third graders enthusiastically and successfully tackle every other task described in this chapter.

The National Archives and Records Administration has regional branches in the following cities, where visitors can search through census records from anywhere in the United States:

Anchorage                        Lee's Summit, MO
Atlanta                          New York City
Bayonne, NJ                      Philadelphia
Chicago                          Pittsfield, MA
College Park, MD                 San Francisco
Dayton                           Seattle
Denver                           St. Louis
Fort Worth                       Suitland, MD
Kansas City, MO                  Waltham, MA
Laguna Niguel, CA

These offices provide resources such as a "Soundex," which indexes names by phonetic sounds rather than only by spelling, since the spelling of names (like everything else in the English language) has varied considerably over the centuries. The Church of Jesus Christ of Latter-day Saints has made genealogy and family history a major endeavor, and its libraries and family history centers throughout the country provide access to detailed records of all kinds. Illinois, for example, has eleven centers. Whatever is not immediately available at a center can be ordered from the church's central library for local viewing.

Why are these records so useful in reconstructing family histories? Of course, they provide information about the person named. Census records name the head of household, spouse and children, and other occupants, and include their ages, places of birth, birthplace of parents of the adults (though not their names), occupations, marital status, and various other information, depending on the state where the census was taken. Death records include the names of the deceased person's parents, as well as where the parents were born. School records provide the name of the child's parent or guardian (in many locations only the male and not the female, unless the male is unknown). The Social Security Death Index, kept since 1937, gives the date of a person's death, which allows the researcher to find a death certificate, which in turn provides information about the previous generation. Newspaper obituaries, or the more frequently created family funeral obituaries such as the one for Pat and Yolanda's ancestor, Katie Parrish Hackworth, often describe the person's activities and accomplishments.

> Obituary of Mrs. Katie Parrish Hackworth
> August 21, 1948
> Coppin A.M.E. Church
> Chicago, Illinois

Katie Parrish Hackworth was born in Aberdeen, Miss., March 11, 1872, the daughter of Emmons and Katie Parrish.

It was at an early age that Katie Parrish realized her inefficiency without the "Heavenly Father" therefore, she confessed Christ and joined the Methodist Church. She went to West Point, Miss., with her Aunt when but a mere lass. After living in the aforementioned town for several years, she met and married the late Ernest Lynwood Hackworth. To this Holy Union, eight children were born—seven of whom survive her.

In the early years of Emmons and Katie Hackworth's married life they moved to Port Gibson, Miss., and there she joined the A.M.E. Church, in which she served faithfully until leaving there after the death of her husband to come to Chicago to be with her children. After being in Chicago but a short time, she joined Coppin A.M.E. Church under the late Rev. A.L. Lindsay, she served loyally until her death Tuesday, August 17, 1948, 8:30 P.M. at Provident Hospital. Her sickness for more than five years was of such nature that she could not attend Church as regularly as she had ofttimes expressed her desire, but whenever she could, never lost an opportunity to be in her Church.

She has left behind a rich heritage of work well done, and a host of friends to mourn her. She was a devoted wife and a loving mother, having reared eight children of her own and three stepchildren.

Her life was one of sunshine, which was beautifully lived in Devotion and Service to all who knew her, and leaves to the memory of her friends a true example of Human Friendship, which they may cherish until the very last syllable of recorded time. She leaves to mourn her passing seven children, three step-children, twenty-one grandchildren, seven great-grandchildren, one sister, one brother, three daughters-in-law, four sons-in-law, several nieces and nephews, and a host of relatives and friends.

"Let us not mourn her going;
Let us rejoice to know
That—earthly labors finished—
She was prepared to go."

"Let us emulate her virtues,
That men of us may say:
The world is brighter, better,
Because she passed this way."

But how can we help the students whose families have resided in the United States for only a short period? This includes people of a wide range of backgrounds, such as recent immigrants from Bosnia, Afghanistan, and Laos, Hispanic immigrants from Mexico, Puerto Rico, and Central and South America over the past fifty years, and Jewish people whose families may have arrived in the 1930s or 1940s, or the late nineteenth century. Even the latter would have only three or four generations to chart, most of whom would be readily known by a student's grandmother or grandfather. How can we help these students obtain information on their family's lineage in the country from which they traveled?

Fortunately, the Internet has stepped into the breach, and its resources are growing constantly. Many national/cultural organizations have made a project of helping Americans research their roots in the organization's source country. One particularly valuable Web site, Cyndi's List (www.CyndisList.com) provides links to an amazing 39,000 of these resources. Following are just a few categories and examples of sites on Cyndi's List. In fact, for each category, there are many more sites than those listed here, and Cyndi's List covers dozens of countries, ethnic groups, and global regions. Below are some examples.

Under Acadian/Cajun/Creole:

Acadian-Cajun Genealogy and History (www.acadian-cajun.com)
Cajun Clickers Genealogy SIG-Baton Rouge, Louisiana
    (www.intersurf.com)
Encyclopedia of Cajun Culture (www.cajunculture.com)
plus thirty more sites, many on the Canadian branch of this
    cultural heritage.

Under Hispanic, Central and South America, and the West Indies:

The Institute of Genealogy and History for Latin America
    (www.infowest.com/l/lplatt/)

Mexican Genealogy How-to Guide (*www.familytreemaker.com*)
Yahoo! . . . Mexico . . . Genealogy—which leads, in turn, to
Spanish Heritage of South Texas and Northeast Mexico
(*www.geocities.com/Heartland/Ranch/5442*)
Mexico GenWeb Project (*www.rootsweb.com*)
plus twenty-eight more sites related to countries throughout the
region.

Other key sites for pursuing genealogy research include:

LDS (Latter-day Saints) Web site (*www.lds.org/*)
LDS Family History Centers in the USA (lists them)
(*www.everton.com/fhcusa.html*)
National Archival Information Locator (*www.nara.gov/nara/nail.html*)
National Geological Society (*www.ngsgenealogy.org.*)
Roots-L Home Page (*www.rootsweb.com/roots-1*)
US Genweb Project (*www.usgenweb.com*)
Where to Write for Vital Records (*www.pueblo.gsa.gov*)
World Family Tree Project (*www.familytreemaker.com*)

Whether working with microfilm records at a library, a branch of
the National Archives and Records Administration, or a Latter-day Saints
Family History Center, or gathering data on the Internet, you'll need to
prepare your students, showing them how to find the appropriate microfilm records or Internet sites and how to read and interpret the information provided. Be sure to conduct a mini-lesson on this, with examples reproduced on overhead transparencies before your field trip or trip
to the school computer lab, so the time will be used efficiently once
you get there. If your students are sending to local records offices for
documents, you will need to help them write their request letters, and
then plan the unit with several weeks' break so there is time for the responses to come back. Real research like this is not easy or convenient,
but the excitement when the documents arrive in the mail, or turn up
on a roll of microfilm, is worth the effort.

## STEP 5:
## CONNECTING WITH NATIONAL AND WORLD HISTORY— AND INCREASING STUDENTS' CHOICES

Paradoxically, finding answers to the blanks on a genealogical chart
ends up presenting more questions than you started with. As students
take the bait and begin to explore their family's history, they will ask
more questions about the past. Eventually, of course, they arrive at the
limits of living memory or available data. It's important not to view this

as an obstacle. Instead, you've simply reached the point where you can ask students to start thinking *historically*. Depending on your curricular goals, you can pose one or more of the following questions:

1. Which ancestors were born during the Industrial Revolution? The technological age? During a time when most people worked in agriculture?
2. Which ancestors might have served in the Revolutionary War? The Civil War? The Mexican-American War? A war that took place in their country of origin?
3. Which ancestors in this country had the right to vote? In the country your family came from, what rights did citizens have? How was the country governed?
4. How were various minorities treated at the time a particular ancestor lived—in this country, or in the country of your family's origin? How did this affect your family?
5. Did you have ancestors who were working in industry during the birth of the American Federation of Labor? The Industrial Workers of the World?
6. Did you have ancestors living in the South during Reconstruction? (And what *was* Reconstruction?)
7. Were there economic hardships your ancestors lived through (depressions, droughts, floods, food shortages such as the Irish potato famine)?
8. How can we learn more about why your ancestors left their country of origin?

And then, for any of these questions: How can we find out what life was like for your great-grandfather or your favorite uncle's great-great-grandmother when that was happening? Obviously, it's time for a well-prepared trip to the library. Each student can pick one of his or her ancestors, and, using a history text, begin to identify various major historical events and conditions that coincided with that ancestor's life. Contact a librarian at the library your students are visiting, and ask him or her to have on display history and geography books, encyclopedias, and other resources that cover some of the countries and periods the kids have chosen, and that fit their grade level. Most librarians love this sort of assignment, since it requires the skills they're most trained for. Your students will then be able to begin gathering historical information from a history textbook or other material for the particular topic they've chosen.

If you haven't already expanded the choices for study, as your students start this broader historical inquiry you will probably do so now.

Some students may be discovering exciting data about their own ancestors, some may grow fascinated with a particular aspect of their family's cultural or social history, and others may hit dead ends and need help finding an aspect of their family's past that is especially meaningful to them. Some may hit pay dirt in the library, some mainly in the census documents, and some at home in the stories told by grandparents. If you can live with the variety, the flow of information will grow rich and fascinating for everyone.

### A Note on Research with Younger Students

If you are teaching younger students, second, third or fourth graders, say, you will be making adjustments so that the research described in this chapter is at a level the children can handle. Many teachers have been successful at guiding student inquiry in the early grades (good examples can be found in *Learning Together Through Inquiry: From Columbus to Integrated Curriculum*, by Kathy Short et al.). Here are some key strategies that provide the structure the children will need:

- Read aloud from lots of good literature that explores the issues the children will be exploring, to build up their prior knowledge and excite their interest—books about families immigrating from other countries, books about life in earlier time periods, books about children learning from grandparents.
- Organize the children into small groups that share a common interest or a common cultural background, so that they can share their questions, brainstorm ideas, and cooperate on difficult information-gathering tasks.
- Provide readings and information sources yourself, since the children may not yet have the skills or patience for finding research materials. If this project is new for you, you may want to schedule this stage in your family history study to straddle a vacation period, when you'll have enough time to search for the resources. Using small groups will also simplify this task, because you will be searching for readings on a limited number of topics.

## STEP 6:
## STUDENTS SHARE THEIR DISCOVERIES

Students use the information gathered in the kinship charts to start linking their personal history to the history of the country and world.

Mere names of ancestors are replaced by stories and conjectures about ancestors. Gossamer sketches become more rounded and colorful humans, with complicated lives lived out in particular periods of history, in particular places, and under particular circumstances. Sharing this information with classmates in brief presentations at the end of workshop sessions allows everyone in the class to become a history teacher. If there's time, students can write up the information in extended essays; however, informal sharing of what students have learned also offers plenty of shared learning and experience in oral presentation.

# goals and objectives

In the course of completing this stage in the family history project, students will experience research in a far more exciting and meaningful way than often happens in school. This results in greater commitment and perseverance, and thus more real learning of research skills. Students can be expected to:

- gather detailed information from family members on the family's kinship lines;
- learn to use census data and other primary historical documents to obtain information about family ancestors;
- learn to use Internet resources to obtain information about their family's history;
- use a kinship chart to organize information about their family's history;
- use history texts and library resources to learn about particular historical events and conditions that influenced their family's history;
- share knowledge about historical events with other students in the class.

# what we got—reality checks
## THE BEARDEN/WALKER KINSHIP CHART

Once Pat Bearden completed her own kinship chart, her son Robert asked her to help him with his. His chart is shown in Figure 5.4. This was in 1995, when Robert was eighteen and a senior in high school. When Pat and Robert talked to Robert Senior, he explained that his father was born in Memphis, where he himself grew up. Pat and son Robert

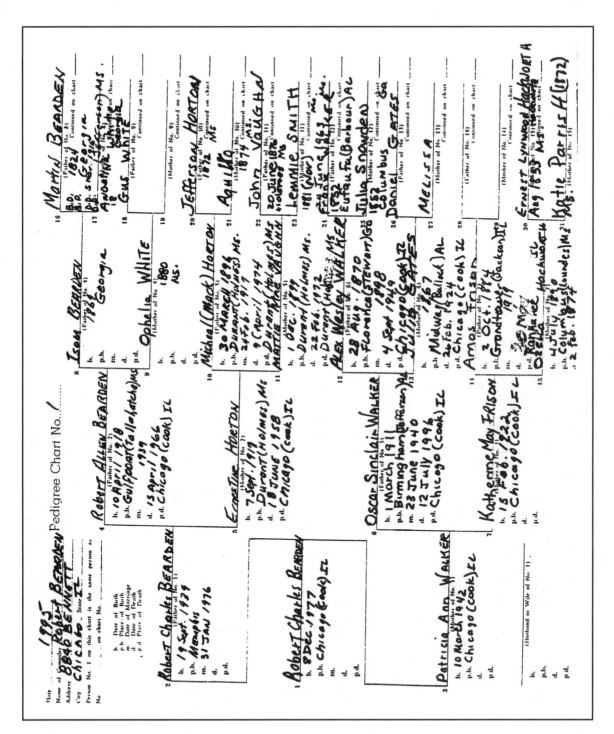

FIGURE 5.4
Robert Bearden's kinship chart

unsuccessfully searched the Memphis records for evidence of the
Bearden family. A second interview, this time with Robert's aunt, re-
vealed that his father was wrong—the grandfather had been born in
Gulfport, Mississippi, and didn't move to Memphis until later in his life.
Once Pat and Robert contacted the state archives office in Jackson, Mississippi, they found information from death index and census records
that took them back several generations further. The Bearden kinship
chart includes the following place names: Chicago, Illinois; Gulfport,
Mississippi; Memphis, Tennessee; Durant, Mississippi; Birmingham, Alabama; Florence, Georgia; Midway, Alabama; Grandtower, Illinois; and
Columbus, Mississippi. The dates go back as far as 1824. Robert helped
put all the information into the computer and formatted it for publica-
tion in the Bearden family book (some of the documents from which are
reproduced as Figures 5.5 through 5.8).

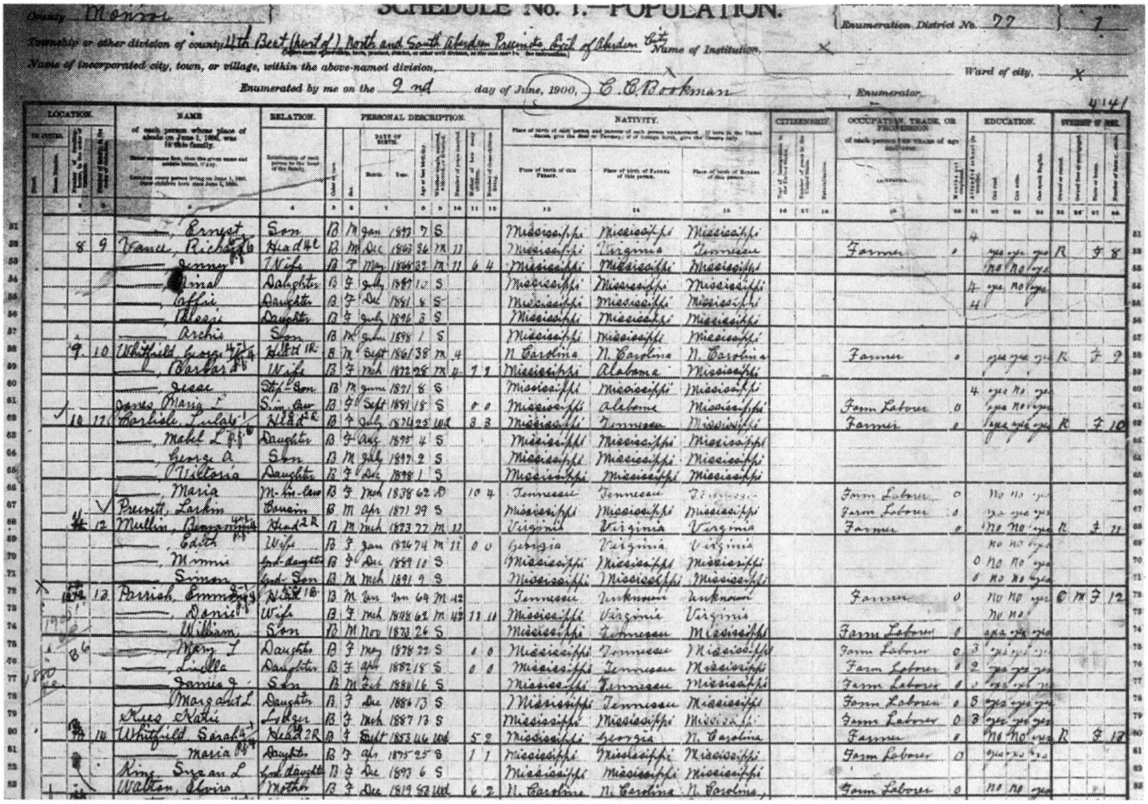

**FIGURE 5.5**
Page from a census tract. Pat Bearden's ancestors, the Parrish family, are listed at the bottom.

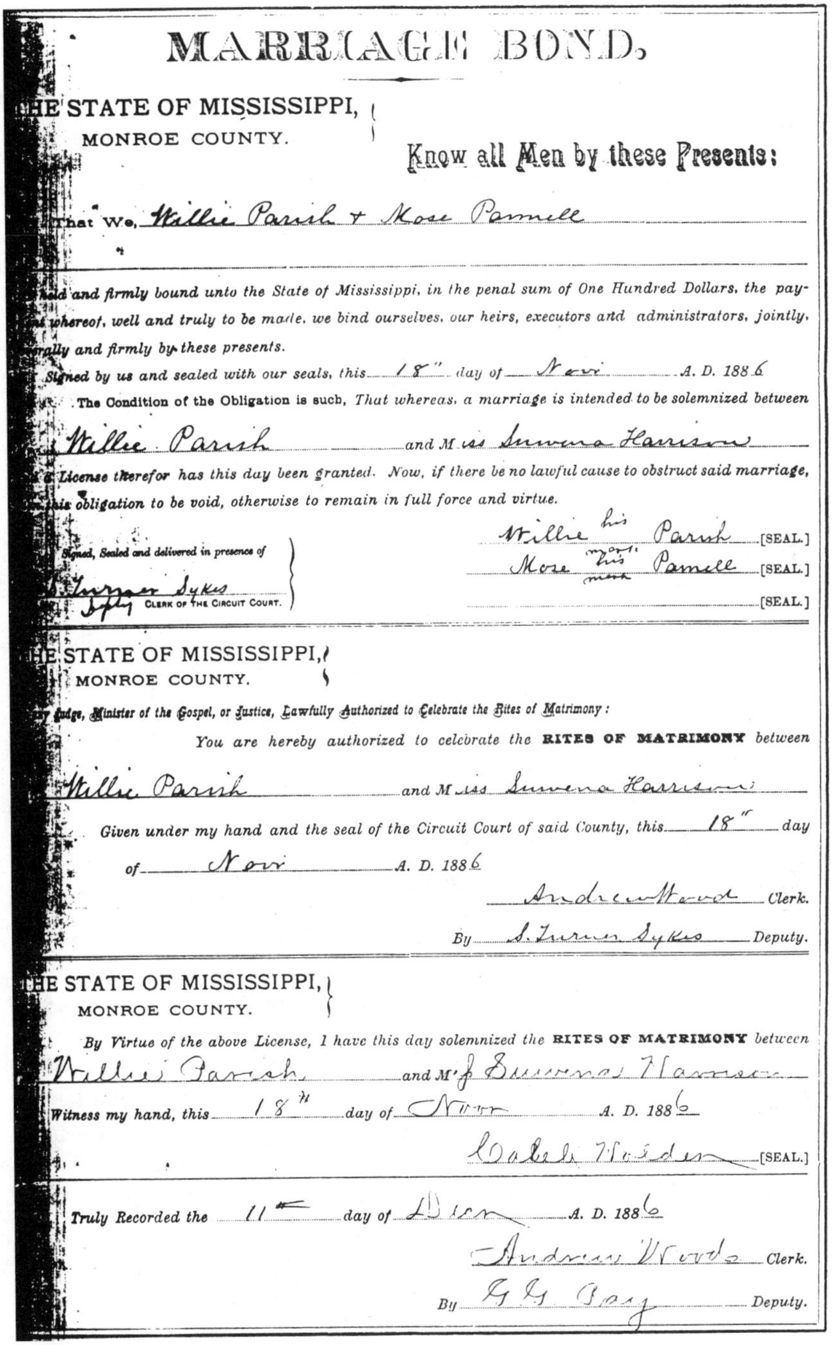

## MARRIAGE BOND,

**THE STATE OF MISSISSIPPI,**
MONROE COUNTY.

**Know all Men by these Presents:**

That We, *Willie Parish + Mose Pannell*

and firmly bound unto the State of Mississippi, in the penal sum of One Hundred Dollars, the payment whereof, well and truly to be made, we bind ourselves, our heirs, executors and administrators, jointly, severally and firmly by these presents.

Signed by us and sealed with our seals, this *18" day of Nov* A. D. 188 *6*

The Condition of the Obligation is such, That whereas, a marriage is intended to be solemnized between

*Willie Parish* and M iss *Suwena Harrison*

License therefor has this day been granted. Now, if there be no lawful cause to obstruct said marriage, this obligation to be void, otherwise to remain in full force and virtue.

Signed, Sealed and delivered in presence of }

*Turner Sykes*
CLERK OF THE CIRCUIT COURT.

*Willie* his *Parish* [SEAL]
*Mose* his *Pannell* [SEAL]
[SEAL]

**THE STATE OF MISSISSIPPI,**
MONROE COUNTY.

Judge, Minister of the Gospel, or Justice, Lawfully Authorized to Celebrate the Rites of Matrimony :

You are hereby authorized to celebrate the **RITES OF MATRIMONY** between

*Willie Parish* and M iss *Suwena Harrison*

Given under my hand and the seal of the Circuit Court of said County, this *18"* day of *Nov* A. D. 188 *6*

*Andrew Wood* Clerk.

By *S. Turner Sykes* Deputy.

**THE STATE OF MISSISSIPPI,**
MONROE COUNTY.

By Virtue of the above License, I have this day solemnized the **RITES OF MATRIMONY** between

*Willie Parish* and M *rs Suwena Harrison*

Witness my hand, this *18"* day of *Nov* A. D. 188 *6*

*Isabel Woeden* [SEAL]

Truly Recorded the *11* day of *Dicr* A. D. 188 *6*

*Andrew Woods* Clerk.

By *G. G. Bay* Deputy.

FIGURE 5.6
Marriage certificate for William Parrish and his wife, Suwena

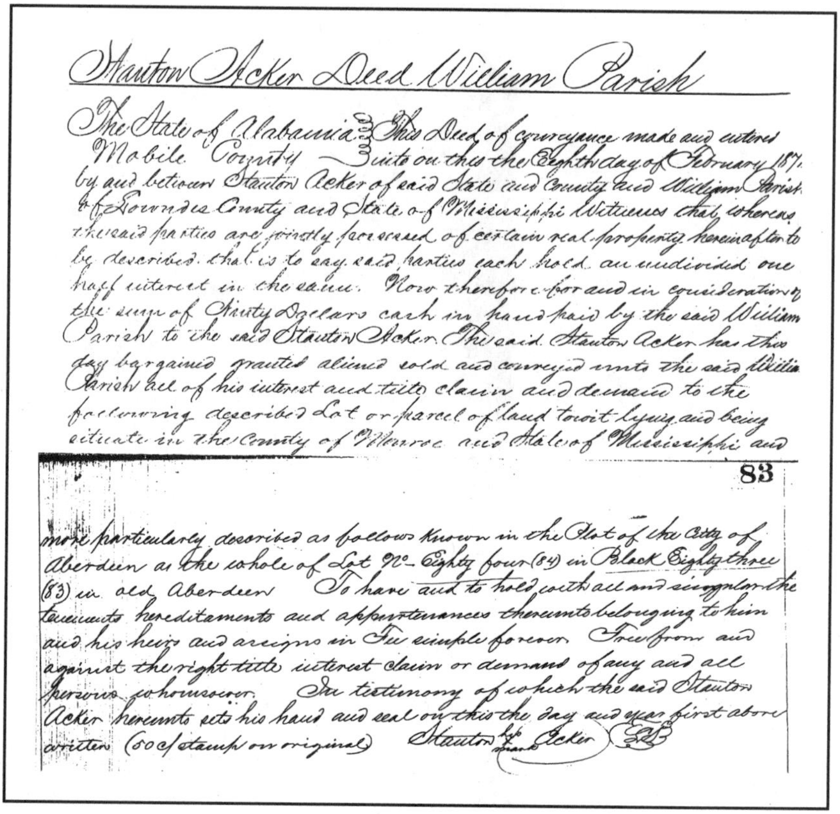

Stanton Acker Deed William Parish

The State of Alabama } This Deed of conveyance made and entered
Mobile County } into on this the Eighth day of February 187[illegible]
by and between Stanton Acker of said State and County and William Parish
of Lowndes County and State of Mississippi Witnesses that whereas
the said parties are jointly possessed of certain real property hereinafter to
be described. that is to say said parties each hold an undivided one
half interest in the same. Now therefore for and in consideration of
the sum of Thirty Dollars cash in hand paid by the said William
Parish to the said Stanton Acker. The said Stanton Acker has this
day bargained granted aliened sold and conveyed unto the said William
Parish all of his interest and title claim and demand to the
following described Lot or parcel of land towit lying and being
situate in the County of Monroe and State of Mississippi and

83

more particularly described as follows Known in the Plat of the City of
Aberdeen as the whole of Lot No. Eighty four (84) in Block Eighty three
(83) in old Aberdeen To have and to hold with all and singular the
tenements hereditaments and appurtenances thereunto belonging to him
and his heirs and assigns in Fee simple forever. Free from and
against the right title interest claim or demand of any and all
persons whomsoever. In testimony of which the said Stanton
Acker hereunto sets his hand and seal on this the day and year first above
written (50c/stamp on original) Stanton his mark Acker (L.S.)

FIGURE 5.7
Deed to William Parrish

## THE LEKI/ALBANO KINSHIP CHART

Eli Leki's Leki/Albano kinship chart, seen in Figure 5.9, includes the place names: Chicago, Illinois; Przedmieczie Dubiesko, Poland; Katowicz, Poland; Divernon, Illinois; and Naples, Italy. The dates go back as far as 1892. The staggering events of twentieth-century Europe and the world can be explored by placing Eli's great-great-grandparents in their historical context. At the Sunflower Cooperative School in Chicago, this is exactly what was done. Eli's source for primary information was his grandmother Nina Leki, who shared stories with him about her village life in Poland between the two world wars. Nina's father was drafted into the Prussian army during the First World War, was captured by the Russians, lost his teeth while held prisoner, and contracted tuberculosis

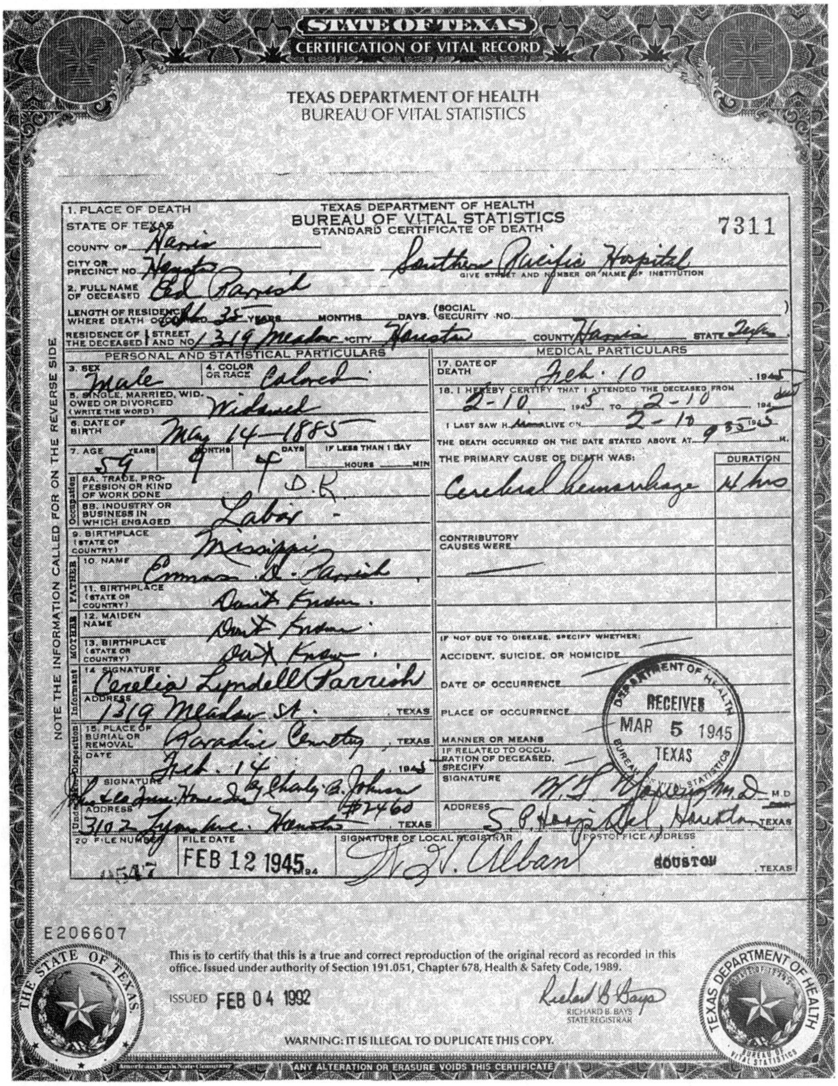
STATE OF TEXAS
CERTIFICATION OF VITAL RECORD
TEXAS DEPARTMENT OF HEALTH
BUREAU OF VITAL STATISTICS

TEXAS DEPARTMENT OF HEALTH
BUREAU OF VITAL STATISTICS
STANDARD CERTIFICATE OF DEATH
7311

1. PLACE OF DEATH
STATE OF TEXAS
COUNTY OF Harris
CITY OR PRECINCT NO. Houston — Southern Pacific Hospital (GIVE STREET AND NUMBER OR NAME OF INSTITUTION)
2. FULL NAME OF DECEASED Ed Parrish
LENGTH OF RESIDENCE WHERE DEATH OCCURRED 35 YEARS MONTHS DAYS. (SOCIAL SECURITY NO. )
RESIDENCE OF THE DECEASED STREET AND NO. 1319 Meadow CITY Houston COUNTY Harris STATE Texas

PERSONAL AND STATISTICAL PARTICULARS
3. SEX Male
4. COLOR OR RACE Colored
5. SINGLE, MARRIED, WIDOWED OR DIVORCED (WRITE THE WORD) Widowed
6. DATE OF BIRTH May 14 1885
7. AGE 59 YEARS 9 MONTHS 4 DAYS — IF LESS THAN 1 DAY HOURS MIN
8A. TRADE, PROFESSION OR KIND OF WORK DONE D.K.
8B. INDUSTRY OR BUSINESS IN WHICH ENGAGED Labor
9. BIRTHPLACE (STATE OR COUNTRY) Mississippi
10. NAME (FATHER) Emmas D. Parrish
11. BIRTHPLACE (STATE OR COUNTRY) Don't Know
12. MAIDEN NAME (MOTHER) Don't Know
13. BIRTHPLACE (STATE OR COUNTRY) Don't Know
14. SIGNATURE (INFORMANT) Cecelia Lyndell Parrish
ADDRESS 1319 Meadow St. TEXAS
15. PLACE OF BURIAL OR REMOVAL Paradise Cemetery, TEXAS
DATE Feb. 14 1945
16. SIGNATURE (UNDERTAKER) Charles B. Johnson #2460
ADDRESS 3102 Lyons Ave. Houston TEXAS

MEDICAL PARTICULARS
17. DATE OF DEATH Feb. 10 1945
18. I HEREBY CERTIFY THAT I ATTENDED THE DECEASED FROM 2-10 1945 TO 2-10 1945
I LAST SAW H ALIVE ON 2-10 1945
THE DEATH OCCURRED ON THE DATE STATED ABOVE AT 9 35 M.
THE PRIMARY CAUSE OF DEATH WAS: Cerebral hemorrhage — DURATION 14 hrs
CONTRIBUTORY CAUSES WERE —
IF NOT DUE TO DISEASE, SPECIFY WHETHER:
ACCIDENT, SUICIDE, OR HOMICIDE
DATE OF OCCURRENCE
PLACE OF OCCURRENCE
MANNER OR MEANS
IF RELATED TO OCCUPATION OF DECEASED, SPECIFY
SIGNATURE M.D.
ADDRESS S. P. Hospital, Houston TEXAS

RECEIVED MAR 5 1945 TEXAS — DEPARTMENT OF HEALTH BUREAU OF VITAL STATISTICS

20. FILE NUMBER 0547
FILE DATE FEB 12 1945
SIGNATURE OF LOCAL REGISTRAR W. D. Alban
POSTOFFICE ADDRESS HOUSTON, TEXAS

NOTE THE INFORMATION CALLED FOR ON THE REVERSE SIDE

E206607
This is to certify that this is a true and correct reproduction of the original record as recorded in this office. Issued under authority of Section 191.051, Chapter 678, Health & Safety Code, 1989.
ISSUED FEB 04 1992
RICHARD B. BAYS
STATE REGISTRAR
WARNING: IT IS ILLEGAL TO DUPLICATE THIS COPY.
THE STATE OF TEXAS
TEXAS DEPARTMENT OF HEALTH — BUREAU OF VITAL STATISTICS
ANY ALTERATION OR ERASURE VOIDS THIS CERTIFICATE

FIGURE 5.8
Death certificate for Ed Parrish

from which he eventually died. Nina described to Eli the plight of Jews and Gypsies under the Nazis, recounting incidents she herself witnessed. By sharing these stories with his classmates, Eli and his grandmother helped them to personally connect to large themes and events in history.

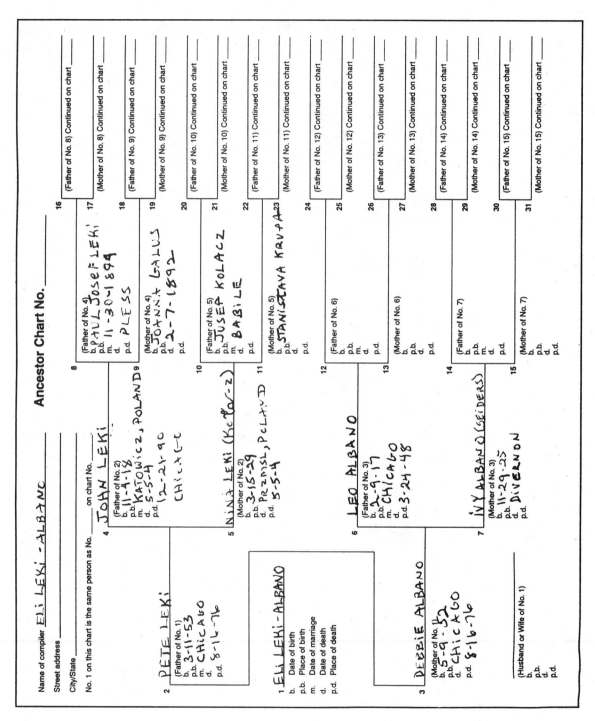

**Ancestor Chart No.**

Name of compiler Eli LEKI-ALBANO

Street address _____

City/State _____

No. 1 on this chart is the same person as No. ___ on chart No. ___

1 Eli LEKI-ALBANO
b.   Date of birth
p.b. Place of birth
m.   Date of marriage
d.   Date of death
p.d. Place of death

2 PETE LEKI
(Father of No. 1)
b. 3-11-53
p.b. CHICAGO
m.
d. 8-16-76
p.d. CHICAGO

3 DEBBIE ALBANO
(Mother of No. 1)
b. 5-9-52
p.b. CHICAGO
d. 8-16-76
p.d.

4 JOHN LEKI
(Father of No. 2)
b. 11-4-18
p.b. KATOWICZ, POLAND
m. 5-5-4
d. 12-21-90
p.d. CHICAGO

5 NINA LEKI (KOLACZ)
(Mother of No. 2)
b. 3-15-29
p.b. PRZMSL, POLAND
d. 5-5-4
p.d.

6 LEO ALBANO
(Father of No. 3)
b. 2-9-17
p.b. CHICAGO
m.
d. 3-24-48
p.d. 3-24-48

7 IVY ALBANO (SEIDERS)
(Mother of No. 3)
b. 11-29-25
p.b. DIVERNON
d.
p.d.

8 PAUL JOSEF LEKI
(Father of No. 4)
b.
p.b.
m. 11-30-1899
p.d. PLESS

9 JOANNA GALUS
(Mother of No. 4)
b.
d. 2-7-1892
p.d.

10 JUSEP KOLACZ
(Father of No. 5)
b.
p.b.
m. BABILE
p.d.

11 STANISLAVA KRVPA
(Mother of No. 5)
b.
d.
p.d.

12 (Father of No. 6)
b.
p.b.
m.
p.d.

13 (Mother of No. 6)
b.
p.b.
p.d.

14 (Father of No. 7)
b.
p.b.
m.
p.d.

15 (Mother of No. 7)
b.
p.b.
p.d.

16 (Father of No. 8) Continued on chart ___

17 (Mother of No. 8) Continued on chart ___

18 (Father of No. 9) Continued on chart ___

19 (Mother of No. 9) Continued on chart ___

20 (Father of No. 10) Continued on chart ___

21 (Mother of No. 10) Continued on chart ___

22 (Father of No. 11) Continued on chart ___

23 (Mother of No. 11) Continued on chart ___

24 (Father of No. 12) Continued on chart ___

25 (Mother of No. 12) Continued on chart ___

26 (Father of No. 13) Continued on chart ___

27 (Mother of No. 13) Continued on chart ___

28 (Father of No. 14) Continued on chart ___

29 (Mother of No. 14) Continued on chart ___

30 (Father of No. 15) Continued on chart ___

31 (Mother of No. 15) Continued on chart ___

(Husband or Wife of No. 1)
b.
p.b.
d.
p.d.

FIGURE 5.9
Eli Leki-Albano's kinship chart

## GLORIA AND TATIANA DAVIS DISCOVER THEIR LINK TO JEFFERSON DAVIS

Gloria Davis, a parent participating in the Family History Parent Project at Jenner Academy, told us that she had called relatives in Mississippi to find out some things for her kinship chart. Her Aunt Florene in Woodville told her, "They got a picture of your great-great-grandmother up in the courthouse." Gloria wondered what it was all about and kept pushing until she learned the wording under the picture, which stated that Farah Davis was the nanny to Jefferson Davis, leader of the Confederacy. Gloria and her eighth-grade daughter Tatiana then looked in an encyclopedia under "Davis, Jefferson" to read more about this person who shares their last name. It says the Southern general's family moved from Kentucky, where he was born, to Woodville, Wilkinson County, near Natchez, Mississippi, in 1810—the same hometown of Gloria's kinfolk.

In the same Parent Project, Cozella Brown insisted, "No use my filling out this chart. I don't have any family. I was raised in an orphanage in Paducah, Kentucky." Nevertheless, after encouragement, she sent a request to the Bureau of Records in Paducah, and three weeks later, she received her parents' birth certificates in the mail. "Cost me ten dollars," she said. On it are named her grandparents, with the dates and places of their birth.

Ms. Brown is the great-grandmother of Raven Gentry, a student at Jenner who was to begin a family history study project that next year. "What's all that for?" Raven asked, pointing to a display of Ms. Brown's photos, documents, stories, and family tree.

"That's your people," Ms. Brown said. "That's gonna belong to you, Raven."

## UPWARD BOUND

In a summer Upward Bound program at Daley Community College, for Chicago high school kids, the students eagerly dove into the work of completing kinship charts and searching census records at the nearby regional office of the National Archives and Records Administration. As the students sat down to work, Maggie Contreras said she had asked her grandfather about their family history. "Where were you born?" she'd asked him. "On the floor," he replied.

You know, 'cause in Mexico a lot of people are born in their homes, not in a hospital. But my grandmother gave me a lot of information. It's a little hard because her and my mother don't get along.

Supposedly her parents moved to Colorado in 1918 to find work. I'm not sure what happened. But all her brothers and sisters were born over there and then they moved back to Mexico. She went back to Mexico in 1931. In 1980 they moved back to the United States.

I hope she doesn't get mad (about asking all the questions).

Maggie told Pete Leki that her forefathers were bricklayers, although her own father "works on the roofs." Her female ancestors were all listed as housewives. "But that's something I don't want to be. I don't want to do that. I was playing volleyball in front of my house with my friends and my mother called. She said, 'You shouldn't be playing ball. You should be inside keeping house.' But I'm not gonna do that."

Pete said, "Well, you can see where that came from, though."

At the archives, Maggie looked up the Soundex card using the code for her grandmother's name, Z530. Dim light, smudged cards through Z328, Z490, Z523, excruciatingly slow, then some out-of-order cards, their numbers going backward. And then, there it was: Francisco Zamudio, in Evans, Colorado. Race was designated by a strange icon, like OT, but smashed together. It gave the enumeration number and other information for pulling the census records.

Again there was a long slow haul to the exact page of the census document, until there, on the top three lines of one page and the bottom line of the previous page, was the Zamudio household. The document showed the same strange smeared race designation (the Zamudios were the only people on either page not listed as W—White). Great-Grandma couldn't read, but the kids could. The immigration date was 1918, just as Maggie had heard. Under "occupation," the document said "field worker"—in the beet fields. Almost all the neighbors were similarly occupied. Interestingly, the Zamudios were the only Mexican household listed; most of the others were German.

Later, we researched the Mexican immigrant experience in the United States and found a wealth of information. A *New York Times* article announced the opening of the U.S.-Mexican border in 1918 to supply agricultural workers to the U.S. beet fields. Census data showed numbers of immigrants involved in the beet fields. We even found a Mexican "Beetfield Workers' Song." We suggested that Maggie read Louise Erdrich's *Beet Queen*, set in the beet fields of Minnesota.

Some of the other students jotted the following observations in their journals:

I ask my mom for most of the information. At first she told me not to bother her, but I told her it was for a project for school. As she was washing the oven, she told me I was asking too many questions, but she answered what she knew. Later, when I was sleeping, she asked my father questions about his family.

In the morning my mom had some names written down for me. After that I asked her about relatives that have come here. She told me I bothered too much, but again she answered. I asked her for any obituaries, birth certificates (I personally looked for them) but found nothing. She told me she didn't know of anyone else who could give me more information.

—DIANA ESCARZAGA

I didn't go into that much information. My dad, mom and an aunt were happy to cooperate with my project. They also told me little stories, such as when my dad came to the U.S. for the first time. He came with my grandfather as "braceros". They also told me that the brother of my great grandmother went to the Mexican Revolution and never came back or was heard from him again. And also that when my dad came that they had to travel in the forest during the cold winter, and they didn't have blankets or heaters to warm up. I also learned that my great grandmother got married when she was only 14 years old.

—JOSE RENTERIA

The first person I talked to was my grandmother. After a while I realized that she wasn't very comfortable talking about it. She told me that she didn't like all those old memories. I tried to contact my grandmother sister because she has all the pictures. She hasn't called me back yet.

—BREONDA BRADIE

Well, today I will relate my experiences I had while I researched my family history. It took a lot of phone calls, questioning and overall time and patience. I began by questioning my parents. They told me everything about themselves and grandparents. My mother knew my great grandparents and I had to call my grandfather in Mexico to find out about my other great grandparents. After a lot of investigation I was able to find a picture of my great-great-great grandmother. I estimated that she was born in about 1830's. I really became interested and was even more amazed when I found out that my great-great aunt was a nun. She was the founder of "Hijos del Sagrado Corazon de Jesus". This was an organization that helped sick or homeless children. I wish to continue my studies in my family history.

—SALVADOR VENEGAS

## A STUDENT LEARNS THE FAMILY HISTORY OF HER NAME

One engaging extension activity we often add at this point in the project is called What's in a Name. Students research the meaning of their name and gather information from family members about its significance. Best Practice High School student Miranda Warren was not able to trace very far on a kinship chart since her family immigrated from Cuba. But she uncovered and reflected upon this moving link with her namesake great-grandmother, teaching us about some rural Cuban cultural beliefs in the process.

### Cuban Blues
by *Miranda Warren*

When I entered my grandmothers old and ancient looking apartment I felt today was different somehow. My grandma never cried in front of us but we knew when she was hurt. She had a look that changed all of my thoughts. Her expression changed mine to look as if I was in a great sorrow. She was very quiet which was abnormal. My grandma originally spoke what was on her mind and what she felt was on the minds of everyone around.

"Hello Mirandy," she said quietly.

"What's wrong Nanna?" I had a feeling she felt the concern in my voice. My grandma is originally from Cuba and she was very into her voodoo religion and the rituals they followed when they were younger. She was a seer in her village which meant she always knew what was going to happen and what everyone else saw. She also thought she always knew what everyone's thoughts were. Most of the time she was right. That was pretty scary to me.

"I jus got mail thad my fadda has jus passed," she said slowly with the first tear in her eye that I have ever seen. "Da curse will now spread. Im is next afta my brotha."

I never really caught on to my grandma's accent until that day. My fathers accent wasn't like hers. She spoke as if she was living back in the iceage. Today her voice sent chills through me. Her words were icy and seemed to sting. She struck a fear deep in me. I should have never asked her "What curse?"

"When I was a young girl my father left for two years. While he was gone my mother had a child. When my father came back he wouldn't speak to no one on my mother's side of the family. See he knew what only the family knew. The baby my mother Miranda gave birth to was not his. Miranda had committed adultery. She never wanted another child. She already had four that never behaved.

"See in Cuba when you commit adultery your spirit is considered to be cursed. When women with cursed spirits give birth their babies are considered dead or zombies. All zombies of any sort were said to bring the cursed spirits to people from the land of the dead. That's why zombies are considered the messengers of the dead.

"My father held his tongue for one year. What he knew was there were only two choices: live with a house full of curses or leave before any of the judges found out. If the judges find out he would have no choice but to send away his family forever or die in their honor. He was very troubled for a while and didn't mention what he knew to his wife.

"Miranda cried herself to sleep every night with the thought of her dead family in her mind. She didn't want the judges to banish her and her children from the village and curse her children's lives. She hadn't told no one but her mother who was very ill and not able to do a lot of things, like talking. A way out was to kill her husband. She loved him but her child was more valuable than her husband. She dreamt it but it couldn't happen like that. She finally knew what she had to do.

"Miranda kissed all four of her children with tears in her eyes. She took the baby and left. When my father got home he went crazy looking for his wife. Since I was the second oldest he had me and my older brother help look for her everywhere.

"My father thought the crazy white colored men who raped the women had took her. So he had his knife with him. When my mother left she had a knife also. Me and my brother were too young to understand the importance in this. We went by the beach to play. The sand was very hot and wet. While running towards the water we noticed the babies blanket was in the water covered with blood. After I saw that I knew my mother would never come back again. That is why I was the seer. There were things I knew at an early age. At that point I knew right away that my life would never be the same.

"My father grabbed the blanket and broke out in tears. The blood on the blanket was burned and so was all of the babies and my mothers things. That would lift all of the evilness from the house.

"Not too long after that the judges found out all about the incident. Miranda's floating body was found on the shore. Her skin was a very pale white. She lost all color in her skin. Her face had a look of anguish and pity.

"The judges put judgment on the family and deemed us all cursed. The curse would pass as each of our spirits passed. Miranda would hunt us in a time in life when we need an answer. That's what my mother needed, an answer. She couldn't find one from anyone. We were also cursed for holding those types of secrets."

By now her old face was filled with tears. I somehow felt her pain. She made me feel as if it was my fault. That's only because I was said to be holding my great-grandmother's spirit. My name made me feel strange for the first time in my life. I wanted to hold my grandma but we are not allowed to touch when tears are in our presence. It's a Cuban ritual.

"Mirandy do me one favor," she looked as if she was pleading for her life. There was a lot of desperation in her eyes. "Don't die with any secrets or regrets on your heart and don't let those regrets kill you."

I promised her I would do her that one favor. She said no one in the family told me because they thought I would overreact because of my name. I feel proud that Miranda tried to protect her family with her own life. I truly respect her decision. If it was me I would do the exact same thing.

As far as the curse is concerned I kind of don't believe it too much. There are a lot of superstitions and I think that is one of them. The warning was very helpful though.

# CHAPTER 6
## Time lines for family and formal history

*O*ur lives stretch back behind us in time. When we reflect on turning points and moments in our lives that we feel were important, we have engaged in one way to consider history. A time line places such moments on a one-dimensional graph, spacing them so that inches help us visually locate events and the stretches between them, within the steady march of time. Our life begins with birth and extends until now, overlapping with the time lines of our parents and grandparents. All of these overlap with the large events that influence our lives. Overlaying personal and family time lines onto formal historic time lines—such as American history 1830–1890, world history 1600–1900, or a specific city or state history—will help to draw your students into an examination of history based on their family's experience.

From the perspective of the traditional curriculum, this is where family history really begins to provide crucial support, helping students to engage with history in ways that most never have before. From our perspective, the personal, the family, and the larger communal history are all important, all equally worth studying in their own right, and worth comparing with one another. In this chapter, we'll explain how to help students create and compare these time lines.

Not only is it valuable to ask students to do this, but when parents come together in groups to do the same work, it offers an opportunity for careful and deliberate sharing between parent and child. Comparing the perspectives of the two (or more) generations helps children become aware of how we all subjectively weigh events and search for the causality and uniqueness of our history.

As you will see, particularly with younger students, there's teaching to do to help children understand the concept that successive lengths along a line can correspond proportionally to successive periods of time. This is a mathematical concept, so we can think about various connections between this activity and the math curriculum. Time line construction involves discrete intervals, concepts of scale, directionality, and positive and negative number values. And then, since a time line is merely a sketch, a set of brief symbolic references to a series of complex events, we can help students choose particular events in their own lives, their family, and wider history to explore and describe so that everyone can understand and appreciate them more fully.

# how-to guide for individual time lines
## STEP 1:
## STEPPING-STONES IN OUR LIVES

Ask your students to spend some time identifying and reflecting on the "stepping-stones" of their lives so far, each jotting down on an index card important moments, big events, changes, tragedies, and achievements that come to their minds, along with approximate dates. What are the key moments, the things that stand out as important when we look back? Invite several volunteers to share some of their moments. Each person's renderings will be different. Some will seem mundane, some tragic, some lighthearted.

## STEP 2:
## TRANSLATION TO A TIME LINE

Pass out some long rectangular paper—eleven by seventeen inches cut in two lengthwise will produce a good size to start with. Ask students to draw a line down the length of the page. On the far righthand side they should draw a dot on the line and label it with the current day's date. Just to its right, have them draw an arrow marked "Future." On the lefthand side, the students draw a dot on the line, mark it "Birth," and write down the date of birth.

Then, let the students go to it. As they enter their special moments on their time line, they will have to organize time in a linear fashion and allow room for all their moments. Many will explore and figure out the concept of intervals. Stress that since this is a working draft, experimentation is inevitable and desirable. Student work will proceed in a variety of forms. Some will bunch events at the beginning of the time line, some at the end. Some will see the need to mark discrete intervals representing years but won't be able to locate the current date neatly at the end of their sheet. Go around the room and ask students to share examples of their progress and difficulties.

By the end of this session, your students should have a draft version of their own personal history time line. Some will be better crafted than others. But even those with asymmetrical and distorted time lines will have entered significant information in a directional pattern, and will have given some shape to their conception of their lives.

### STEP 3:
### A MINI-LESSON ON HOW TIME LINES WORK

Bring in some examples of standard history time lines from textbooks and/or computer software. Hold them up if they're large, or give out copies or show them as overhead transparencies if they're small. Ask the students to comment on them.

- What period of time does each cover?
- How is time represented?
- What time interval is used as the standard? One year? Ten years? One hundred years? One million years?
- What techniques were used to fit information in along the line? What is the linear distance used to represent a given unit of time?

Using a large chalk protractor, divide a line on the board and then repeat using different interval settings. Ask students to suggest what strategies might be used to make a time line "fit" right on a given length of paper. Of course, they'll be using division and geometric multisectioning of a line to solve the problem.

### STEP 4:
### REVISING THE DRAFT TIME LINES

Now ask the students to take their draft time lines home to share with parents or guardians. The children should ask the adults to recall additional events from the same time period as the child's time line and write them on a separate sheet of paper. The student can then decide which ones (if any) to include on his/her working draft time line.

Once these data have been gathered, have students use fresh strips of paper, protractors, rulers, and straightedges to redraw their time lines with standard intervals (i.e., equal increments representing discreet and equal amounts of time). By observing the various strategies students use to develop their own time lines you can gauge their understanding of the mathematical concepts. When the layout is finished, the students can fill in their previously charted events plus the newly gathered items. Finally, ask students to share and explain their work, first in small groups and then several to the whole class. By the end of this workshop, your students should have their second draft, more correctly approximating a to-scale, well-organized, readable life time line.

# how-to guide for family time lines
## STEP 1:
## GATHERING DATA FOR FAMILY TIME LINES

Ask your students to take home their own personal time line once again and ask parents, grandparents, and/or other guardians to dictate a list of important events throughout their own lives and what they know of the lives of *their* parents and grandparents. Students can of course use information already gathered from interviews in previous family history activities (when they asked about immigration to the current home, jobs the immigrants first held, wars participated in, and facts about ancestors for the kinship charts). But this is also an opportunity to learn about additional events that may not have been covered before.

It's a good idea to interview several family members to get different time frames and perspectives. And you may want to model the interview process, using your knowledge of your own family's history, to help students ask about the sorts of things that qualify as stepping stones and turning points:

- births
- marriages
- deaths
- family moves or emigrations
- travels or adventures
- achievements (graduating college, landing a good job, buying a first home)
- tribulations (losing a job, experiencing an illness)
- fighting in or experiencing a war
- participating in a political event or social action

Remind students to obtain dates for the events whenever possible. The students can bring their family information to class as lists on sheets of paper or note cards. Use some of the mini-lessons and tips on interviewing in Chapters 3 and 4 to help students jog their family's memories.

## STEP 2:
## ORGANIZING THE DATA TO CREATE A FAMILY TIME LINE

If students have talked to more than one family member, they'll first need to look over their lists and interweave any overlapping events. They can also bring out their kinship charts as an additional source of information. If they have numerous overlapping lists, it can help to work through them and number the events in one single chronological sequence before writing them on the time line.

Now, starting with one or more fresh strips of paper, each student constructs a time line for his or her family. Students will need to think through a number of decisions. With what date will it start? What important events will be included? How long should it be, physically? If they use the same interval for each year of their family time line as on their own time line, how many sheets of paper will they need?

## STEP 3:
## COMPARING STUDENT AND FAMILY TIME LINES

The point of comparing student and family time lines is to give students an idea of how their own lives fit into the larger context of their family history. Younger children often have little concept of just how long their parents and grandparents have lived. Older students can be helped to picture how their own and their parents' lives are the same and/or different.

If the students have used the same length-to-time scales for their personal and family time lines, they're ready to compare the two. If the two scales are different (perhaps you don't have an endless supply of paper for this project!), the students may need to make a second copy of their personal time line that matches the family version (no doubt a miniature, with a shorter length representing a year). Now students can line up the birth date on the matching student time line with the parents' notation of that child's birth, which should put the time lines in sync. Help your students compare and relate their own lives with the rest of their family. For example, what is the distance between the child's birth year and a parent's birth year? Between the child's birth and a grandparent's? What other family events occurred when one of the parents or grandparents was the same age the child is now?

## STEP 4 (OPTIONAL):
## PRODUCING TIME LINES ON THE COMPUTER

The value of personal and family time lines is in the reflective thinking involved in their construction. These hand drawn lines are unequaled as artifacts of family history. At the same time, a number of computer programs are available to assist in creating formal time lines with great flexibility. Missed events can easily be added after a draft has been completed. The line can be shrunk or expanded on command to fit the linear space available. Text can be printed into flagged boxes. Some students and teachers may prefer this presentation for legibility.

If you have the computer facilities and desire to pursue this step, try using the program titled Timeliner. You'll need time to take students through the tutorial to learn the program before they enter information and print it out as a banner or as a single sheet. Of course, the students can still save the handwritten draft as a more immediate record of their thinking.

## STEP 5:
## COMPARING TIME LINES FOR PERSONAL, FAMILY, AND FORMAL HISTORY

Now we move on to connect family history with more public forms of history. Time lines of events in history are highly limited in the depth of what is presented, because they simply list events without describing or relating them. However, they are very powerful and useful for gaining an overview and placing oneself in time. Many historical time lines are available in CD ROM, texts, and encyclopedias, and they come in a wide variety, covering large or small tracts of time, wide or narrow areas of focus. A teacher who is responsible for covering specific areas of curriculum, say, the Civil War, will be able to access any number of time lines focused on this cataclysm.

Depending on the teacher's range of available options, students can find and select—or compile their own—historical time lines in scale with, and relevant to, their family history time line. For example, if a family time line shows origins back to 1880 in Mississippi, the historical time line could begin with the end of the Civil War and include Reconstruction, the Industrial Revolution, and demographic developments such as the Great Migration from the South and the growth of populations in western territories. Or it could depict inventions and technological changes that may have influenced the family's decision to migrate. Small groups of students can each tackle a different aspect of the period's history, thus making a richer collection of time lines that helps instruct the entire classroom about the period being studied. If these documents are carefully produced and match the family histories in scale, various family and public history pairs can be reproduced as transparencies and then overlapped to vividly show the intersection of historic events with the family chronologies, adding a bold dimension to our methods of helping students grasp the significance of history.

If the class has already studied the particular historical period being considered, you can ask students to speculate about how particular historical events may have looked to their own ancestors and how the events might have affected their lives. If the grandfather didn't fight in a particular war, might he have lost friends who did? Might the growth of particular jobs or cities have influenced the grandmother's decision to move—or was she one of the people who stayed behind?

## STEP 6:
## A TIME LINE NARRATIVE

The time line tells a story about the family's history. But in its bare-bones form, it is only a skeleton of a story. Writing a narrative, using the time line or some part of it as an outline, puts some meat on the bones and blood in the veins. The points on the time line pose questions that want to be answered.

Ask your students to pair up and show each other their personal and family time lines. Each takes a turn, and the speaker chooses a chunk of one time line about which he or she knows a fair amount. The speaker explains it to the listening partner. The listening student then asks follow-up questions about each point. For example:

- Where did you live when you were born?
- Why did you move?
- What jobs did your parents have at that time?
- Do you remember when your little brother was born?
- What was it like going to that school?
- Do you remember a favorite teacher?
- What larger historical events were taking place at the same time?
- How might these have affected you or the family member you are telling about?

Have the students take notes. Using the time line as an outline, and the questions as prompts, your students can now write a narrative about a part of one of their time lines.

## goals and objectives

In completing the personal and family time lines, your students have:

- used their own personal life histories to explore important moments in their lives;
- worked with the mathematical concepts associated with number lines, particularly directionality and intervals, and applied these to their own lives and families;
- gained skill in producing to-scale time lines;
- interacted with their parents or other family members and involved them in a discussion in which the adults are helpful sources of important information;
- studied significant events of public history and made the connection between that history and their own;
- produced powerful presentational forms and valuable family documents;
- practiced some prewriting techniques, shared their time lines with collaborative friends, practiced going from outline to narrative, and added another piece and style of writing to their writing portfolio.

If you used a computer application, your students will have learned a new computer skill and new methods for presenting chronological information.

## reality checks
### PARENT TIME LINES

Kathy Ellis, a parent volunteer at Jenner School, constructed her first time line on a large sheet of paper. The explanations of the important dates were impossibly crammed into one small part of the paper. Kathy returned to the parent room several times to work on and add to the time line. She redrew it on a larger scale and figured out a scheme using lines and arrows to allow her to write down many events in a small space. The current document, Figure 6.1, is a masterpiece of intentional, complex reflection on her life. After her birth in New Orleans, it includes "picked sugar cane," "Mother passed from cancer," "twins born," and all the dates her children entered and left school.

Cozella Brown, great-great-grandparent to Raven Gentry, a fifth

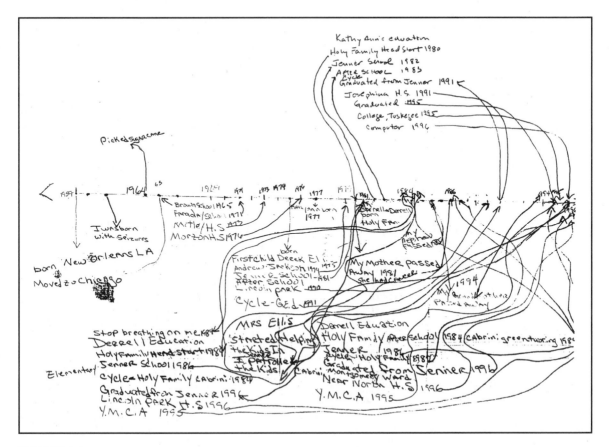

**FIGURE 6.1**

Time line for Kathy Ellis, parent at Jenner School

grader at Jenner, began her time line with the date 1929. By the time she had finished, taped together, and laminated it, it stretched thirty feet long. It included dozens of short vignettes about life in an orphanage, the birth of her child, her first automobile. Taken all together, it could be considered a book of stories about Cozella's life. Part of it is shown in Figure 6.2.

## PETE LEKI'S TIME LINE NARRATIVE

My mother was born on March 15, 1929, outside the small Polish village of Przedmieczie Dubiesko in Przemysl, a county in southeastern Poland. They farmed a tiny family plot in the San River valley. To the south the Carpathian Mountains rose, separating them from the Balkan states of Hungary, Romania, and Czechoslovakia.

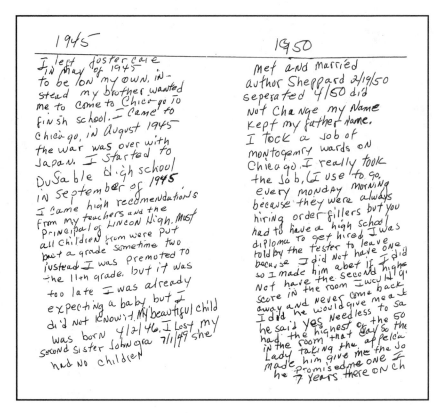

**FIGURE 6.2**

Close up of portion of time line by Cozella Brown, Jenner School parent

They grew potatoes, cabbage, and beets, and grew and spun hemp for clothing. Their house was grass-roofed and dirt-floored. My grandfather Jusef Kolacz came from a family of six brothers who lived just to the east of my mother's village. All the brothers had been drafted into the Austrian army to fight in World War I. He'd spent time in a Russian prison camp, caught consumption, lost his teeth. He was sick all the time. He worked as a cobbler and married into the land of my great-grandfather Antonio Krupa.

My grandfather drank too much. He died on the road to the village in 1939, when my mother was ten years old. Before that, Antonio had died of an infection when my mom was six. That left my grandmother Stanislava Krupa, my mother, and her brother and sister to care for themselves on the farm. My mother remembers her mother as tiny, energetic, and full of love. "Kisses were our Band-Aids," my mother told me.

The war came, and in 1940 the village was occupied by the German Nazis. They demanded conscript labor to run their factories. They took my mother away from her home in 1943 when she was fourteen. She spent the night in the village jail and then was sent with others by wagon to Przemysl. They were put on a train to Berlin and then to Braunsweig, Germany.

She was put to work in a canning plant, then packing sugar, and finally in a scrap metal foundry. She worked there until Allied tanks roared through and the war ended. Then she was placed in a Displaced Persons camp run by the Red Cross in Braunsweig. This is where she met my father. She was sixteen. He was twenty-six.

Pete's time line linked to the narrative is shown in Figure 6.3.

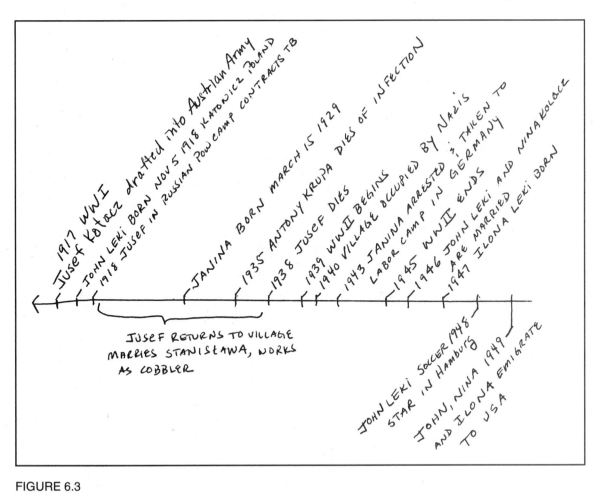

**FIGURE 6.3**

Time line for Janina Leki until she emigrated to this country

## THE DECADES/FAMILY HISTORY PROJECT AT SALINE MIDDLE SCHOOL, SALINE, MICHIGAN

Eighth-grade teachers Suzanne Brion (English), Barbara Bureau (special education), David Fiske (science), and Brian Lampman (social studies) at Saline Middle School have developed a broad integrated study unit that brings many parts of the family history project together to help history come alive for their students. The unit centers around family oral history, personal, family, and historical time lines, and "I-search" projects in which students learn about historical topics of their own choosing. The project spreads out over many weeks, and the kids become highly involved with its many segments as the teachers alternate between project activities and other material they are required to cover.

As a first step, students interview parents and grandparents about their histories to learn the facts of their family's original immigration to the United States, and to create personal and family time lines. This is the most immediate, family-focused portion of the unit. Then, over a period of several weeks, the students gather information for the formal history time lines by working in groups, with each group in charge of a particular level of history—global, national, state, or local. This is the most formal, public-history portion of the project.

Each group must decide upon the ten most outstanding events for each century, at their level, to be placed on the time line. To help students make these choices, the teachers gather history time line books from the school library. Frank Wallis's *Ribbons of Time: World History Year by Year Since 1492* is a favorite. The groups' completed time lines, color-coded for the global-to-local level of the events, are posted on the classroom wall. Individual and family time lines are mounted close by to facilitate comparisons. See Figure 6.4 for examples.

Now students' own decision making and goal setting becomes central. Each student selects a broad topic of interest related somehow to his or her own family experience. Topics range through literature and the arts, sports and entertainment, science, politics, and government. Each student also selects a decade and person or event that influenced the course of history, within the topic of his or her interest. The student must then inquire into that piece of history, learn about it, and determine how it affected his or her own family. This third part of the project, in other words, creates the bridge between family and formal history and builds on students' growing ability to make choices and work independently. Students write essays, create visuals, and prepare statistical depictions about what they've learned. As a further integrating step, students who have focused on the same decade pool their information to

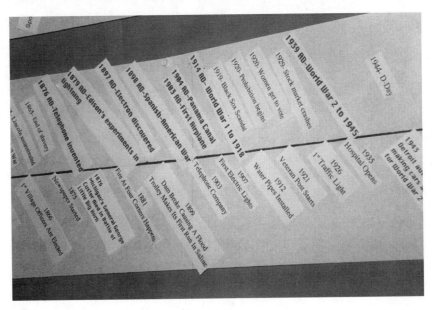

FIGURE 6.4

Time lines in the eighth grade at Saline Middle School

write a group abstract about it. Finally, later in the year, students create three- to eight-minute stage productions to dramatize the events of their chosen decades.

The following are some typical student research essays:

## The Alaskan Gold Rush: The Klondike
### by *Kathryn Beyer*

*"Gold! Gold! Gold! Gold! Sixty-Eight Rich Men on the Steamer Portland. Stacks of Yellow Metal!"* This was the headline of *The Seattle Post-Intelligencer* on July 17, 1897 declaring officially that gold had been discovered in and around the upper Yukon River, the Klondike. With the California Gold Rush, which was 40 years earlier, still on their minds, thousands and thousands of people fled to that remote area. They were mostly young men between the age of 20 and 30.

Most of the new prospectors had no idea where they were going so they went to the Alaskan coast. Soon most of them would take a steamship through the Inland Passage to Skagway or Dyea and then hike to the Klondike via the Chilkoot or White Pass. Once over the pass, they would build boats and float down to Dawson City.

During those days, there were many thieves and criminals. They would gladly release the gold-crazed people of their hard found gold. One man in Skagway was well known and almost ruled Skagway. Jefferson Randolph "Soapy" Smith had a saloon where he did everything from rigging cards to simple pick-pocketing to get money.

Anyone who entered the Yukon had to bring many supplies. Police made people bring at least a years worth of food or 2,000 pounds. This cost about $500 in Seattle and much more closer to the Klondike. Guidebooks recommended many other things such as a tent, a shovel, and a frying pan. The Canadian Government saw this gold rush as a big investment so one of the things they did was place duties on supplies imported from the U.S. The prices raised tremendously such as oranges and lemons went from 50 cents to $1.30. Champagne went from $20 to $40 for a pint.

The conditions of living were horrible in Dawson City. Lots of people lived in tents that were cramped and didn't have heat. Some were lucky enough to have cabins, but in the winter they had to be heated at all times and in the summer there were a ton of mosquitoes making people feel not at all like they were in heaven.

The food was bland or spoiled and nerves were at the point of breaking all the time.

Most of the people that went to the Gold Rush never got rich as they planned. Most ended up hungry and poor in the middle of nowhere. Those who did get rich soon lost it. Lots spent it on beer and dancing halls. Some of the ones who struck it rich became an alcoholic, married a dance-hall girl, blew his cash away, got divorced and died penniless in San Francisco. The only people who really prospered were the merchants and the thieves.

The Gold Rush in the Klondike ended when gold was discovered in Nome, on the Bering Sea, in the summer of 1899.

The Klondike gave lots of gold. In 1896, it produced $300,000 worth of gold. In 1897, it produced $2,500,000, in 1899 it produced $16,000,000, and in 1900 it produced $22,275,000. Gold at the time was worth about $16 an ounce. This made it the largest gold mine ever.

To me the Alaskan Gold Rush was very important. It migrated people to Alaska, it gave people an adventure and it proved that Alaska wasn't just a hunk of ice. Many people learned important lessons in the Klondike. It is also important to me personally because two of my relatives, George Irving Reeves and Richard Edward Reeves, were there and actually dug up gold. They didn't pay for their own trip, but they made a difference in their own lives and others. Because my relatives went there, it has affected my whole family for many reasons. We have many artifacts such as my great grandmother's wedding ring which was made from Alaskan gold. My grandmother has been there lots of times and she co-wrote a book about it which had to have taken a great quantity of time, and my brother and I really want to go to Alaska. I don't know why my brother does but I want to go to see the sites that were seen nearly 100 years ago by my ancestors.

"The Spell of the Yukon"
I wanted the gold and I sought it.
I scrabbled and mucked like a slave.
Was it fame or scurvy—I fought it,
I hurled my youth into the grave.
I wanted the gold and I got it.
Came out with a fortune last fall,
Yet somehow life's not what I thought it.
And somehow the gold is not all.
By Robert Service

## My Family History
### by *Shreena Patel*

During the 1900s–1940s Great Britain ruled India (Hindustan). During this period of time, on my dad's side my great-grandfather, Chaturbhai Patel protested with Mahatma Gandhi, the man who gained India's independence back by using nonviolent methods. My great-grandfather was put in jail for two and a half years in Yarwada jail in Pune because of protesting. As a result of racial discrimination the British took over everything.

One of the things they took over was India's cloth. India's cloth was imported to Britain and then was manufactured and was sent back to India to sell to the Indians. Gandhi encouraged the people to homespin their own cotton. When my great-grandfather was in jail the British soldier forced him to weave the cloth. My great-grandfather then said to the soldiers that he had poor eyesight to weave. During this time my grandmother was about five or six years old.

My dad's side of the family is politically active. My other great-grandfather, Mothibhai Patel was the leader of the village a bit like a mayor. I also found out he was on the British people's side even though he was himself an Indian. My grandmother and grandfather used to be part of the village council where they would make decisions on any village issues and would discuss how to improve the village.

If it wasn't for Gandhi and other people who supported him like my great-grandfather I would still face racial discrimination today and anywhere I go. I will also have certain rules to follow and obey at all times. I am proud of my family. I am also hoping to discover and research more information about the letters that Gandhi wrote to my great-grandfather.

## Feldkamp Relation in History
### by *John Feldkamp*

In the 1920s, the Great Depression occurred. Relatives from both of my parents felt its effect. During 1920 and 1921, the prices of farm products dropped down to forty percent of their original value and stayed there throughout the two years. My Grandma Haynes' parents lost so much money that they had to mortgage their farm. Luckily, during this time, my Grandma Feldkamp's parents had a farm and did not lose it. They even got all of their money out of the bank before it closed. Other farmers were not as fortunate as they were.

Today, other farmers are losing their farms because it just does not make a living for their family as it did before. Being a farmer is the hardest job that I know of. People just do not respect the fact of how hard a person must work to feed his family, along with providing food for others. People back in the 1920s probably had a better idea of how a farm worked than people do now. People do not realize that the grocery store is not the place where food is made. Almost every kind of food that people eat comes from farm products. Eggs, vegetables, bread, cereal, and meat are just a few to mention. With the decrease of farms in the world, there will be less food available for the people to buy. Prices will go up, and food will cost more. If America still wants to be the best country in the world, then it needs to be able to maintain the number of farms.

In the 1920s, America's farms were able to struggle through. Maybe right now is also a struggling time for them. Possibly in a few years, America will pull through and will be well supplied with goods. People should know and care more about the farmers who raise their food, or else maybe they will no longer have it anymore.

The teachers reflect on the success of the project:

Students resonate to this project. Once they begin to research events and people who changed the course of history, and "fit" their family history with public history, they begin to see the connections. Often the connections of an event spark the student's interest in a particular topic. One student used her Japanese mother as the springboard for further investigation of the Japanese internment; another two students were comparing famous relatives only to discover that one was related to Lincoln, and the other was related to Booth. Students who share the Saline German farm family heritage are concerned about the vanishing farmland in the area. One student indicated she was beginning to understand "where her grandparents were coming from" after learning how the depression affected their family when they lost their farm.

This marks the fourth year of our interdisciplinary team project. Each year has seen revisions and improvements. Students see the connections among the disciplines (language arts, social science, science) better and have a deeper understanding of how "history" affected their family and how it influences them. History ceases to be a subject area and becomes his-story/her-story/our story/the story of us and US.

(Special thanks to the following students who helped the teacher team prepare to share this material with us: Lisa Adkins, Kathryn Beyer, Katie Burnett, Joanna Davis, Jana Feldkamp, John Feldkamp, Taryn Hartman, Heather Huizenga, Blake Kramer, Jeanette Marks, Ben Nichols, and Shreena Patel.)

# CHAPTER 7
## Making two-minute videos

*a*fter all the work your students have put into the family history project, they'll probably want something to take home when it's over, something they can share with family members. Also, it's a good idea to have a way to reflect on what people have learned, what it all adds up to mean. Of course, the student papers, the time lines, and the posters for a family history fair are all great keepsakes, tributes to their family members as well as evidence of schoolwork well done. But one challenge for teachers is how to make use of more up-to-date video technology without a long, time-consuming process of training, planning, rehearsing, shooting, and editing. We're offering a quick, easy-to-produce technique we call the two-minute video.

The two-minute video allows each student to recontextualize the materials he or she has compiled during the family history project, to look for central threads that link family with broader social and political history, and to tell about these while displaying the evidence visually. The student writes a script that narrates the family's story and explains the student's learning process. The student then reads the script to accompany short video takes of documents and graphics that he or she created and assembled during the project. Each video is thus completed in one single, short session. Students who are next in line quietly prepare their materials, arranging them on tables and posting them on a classroom wall, getting ready for their turn before the camera. A copy of the video is made for each student so that it can be shared with the family through the coming years.

## how-to guide
### STEP 1:
### ASSEMBLING THE MATERIALS AND REFLECTING UPON THEM

Have the students gather all the materials they've collected and created for the family history project—photographs, primary and secondary sources, census records, birth and death certificates, kinship and occupation charts, maps of migration trails, deeds, time lines, obituaries, interview transcripts, and letters. You'll need to clear lots of space around the classroom. Some students can spread their materials out on tables, while others tape theirs up on walls or bulletin boards. Hallways just outside the classroom will probably have to be pressed into service. Each student needs to have his or her own space. The students shouldn't worry yet about arranging things nicely—just have them get it all on the wall or on a table.

Students should spend some time looking over their materials. Now that they've got all this, encourage them to see it with fresh eyes. What story is being told here? What forces have brought their family to this place, here and now? What are some things they have come to realize about their family now that they've done all this work? About themselves? About their own connections or breaks with the past? About their family's place in the history of this country? What most surprised them as they gathered their information? This is important reflection time, and students can get started by writing a journal entry explaining two or three things they think about differently as a result of the whole project.

### A Mini-Lesson (or Two) on Reflection

It's easy for us to suggest that the teacher invite students to reflect. But in many schools and classrooms, students are accustomed to completing work and moving on, without stopping to think too much about what they've achieved or how, what the most effective strategies were, or how they overcame obstacles. For younger children in particular, reflection is not yet something that occurs to them unbidden. For example, when one third-grade teacher asked students to write about what they'd learned as a result of their family history investigations, the children simply repeated some of the facts they'd gathered. Yet research on effective readers tells us that habits of metacognition are essential. Good readers pose questions to themselves as they read. They decide what's most important in the material, and they monitor their own understanding.

So if you find that at first your students don't have a lot to write in their journals when you ask them to reflect on the family history project, take it as a cue to do some important teaching. And don't be surprised if you find you need to teach the concept in a number of different ways over a period of time. First, *model* reflection yourself, jotting your own journal entry on a blank overhead as the students watch. Talk through the process, emphasizing ways that your own understanding changed as you helped students with the family history project.

You can also provide students with key words and questions that help them see their learning in larger terms:

♦   What new *connections* have I made between different kinds of ideas?
♦   How do I *see* something or someone *differently* than I did before?
♦   How have I *changed* as a result of the things I've learned?

Finally, watch for and read aloud examples of self-reflection in other literature or essays that you and your students may be reading.

## STEP 2:
## CREATING A SCRIPT

Students can start with one or two of the strongest ideas from their reflection journal entry, and then decide which of the documents and visuals that they've assembled relate most directly to these ideas. Which family story best illustrates or connects with these ideas? What facts and events of public history are involved? Each student then writes a script that explains these things, working the story around the documents and other visuals spread out before him or her. Remind the students that two minutes is really a very short time—about 250 words is the most that can be read at a deliberate pace in two minutes. This means each student will be able to share just one strong idea, illustrated with one brief story.

To enrich the visual side of the videos, make available history and social studies texts, copies of *National Geographic,* and vivid art and photography books related to the historical topics your students have investigated. Let your students browse through them to find extra graphics, photos of places, scenes of migrations, wars, farms, famous events, and so on that might help their stories come alive.

Video is a visual medium. Students will need to decide the sequence in which their materials are shown. Each chunk of script (phrase, sentence, or paragraph) should be marked to indicate what the camera will be focusing on for that time period. Students should decide and make notes on how to frame each visual image for the best impact. If a video filmmaker is available to offer suggestions, invite her in for a workshop.

Once first drafts are done, students can review and help refine each other's scripts. Have them ask each other questions:

- Is the script concise?
- How does it link personal and public history?
- Does it have a powerful final statement?
- Are the graphic images striking?
- Do they amplify the text?

Students can motivate each other to write with strength and passion if they give feedback promoting well-written scripts. The final shot can contain a summing-up message; it can show a photograph of the narrator, or a live shot. Opening and closing "boards" with the title and credits can be accompanied by musical tracks linked to the story. The techniques are easy enough to master so that students can do several versions of their story as their research develops.

## STEP 3:
## REHEARSAL AND PRODUCTION

Have the students rehearse for each other, practicing the script a few times, pausing between each take. Then they go ahead to actually produce their films. In this style of video filmmaking, your students can pause the camera between each take to take a breath, repractice a line, and move the camera to the next image. If no experienced filmmaker is available, the camera can be run by teams of two or three students, each taking turns and helping each other. Students should practice framing each video shot. When they are ready, the camera is set to record, and then put on "pause" between shots to allow time to be reset on a new image. There is no post-editing. Students can take their time between shots, but they won't be able to edit out mistakes. The highest quality should be sought for every take. But small errors are inevitable and should be taken in stride. These videos are works-in-progress, and one loses the spirit of the experience if hours and hours are spent reshooting takes. In the interest of the whole group, one time through is all each student gets.

## goals and objectives

When your students create two-minute videos, they will have accomplished the following:

- Reflected on the many things they've learned studying family history.
- Planned a visual representation focusing on a part of their family history.
- Composed a concise, organized script.
- Revised the script, working with peers.
- Orally presented the script.
- Created a permanent visual record of a part of their learning for their families.

## reality checks

Although the following experience took place with high school students, many teachers have conducted successful two-minute video projects with elementary school kids. Pat, Yolanda, and Pete were asked to conduct a family history unit for the Upward Bound program for high school students from the Chicago Public Schools, which took place at Daley Community College on the city's southwest side. The family history component was a short one, but we were determined to include the two-minute video in the curriculum. We asked students to bring whatever they had assembled in their four class sessions and trip to the National Archives, and start writing scripts.

A digression on how ideas grow when people embark on this sort of project: Pat, Yolanda, and Pete all shot demonstration videos for the students to give them an idea of what the project could be like. Pete's video ran two minutes and thirty seconds. Pat and Yo's was ten minutes. A ten-minute two-minute video. Overachievers from the start, they'd stayed up until 3:00 A.M. the night before, writing the script. In fact, the writing process gave birth to a new discovery about the Smith-Parrish family history, ground they'd thought was already well plowed. Their video focused on Monroe County, Mississippi, and what the neighborhood became like after Emancipation, when slave owner and slave lived on the same block.

Later on, Pat and Yo decided this should have been three or four separate two-minute videos. The script-writing process had worked its way into a fissure, a runnel, and then a ravine, opening up on unexplored new territory. It is the researcher's and writer's obligation to search out these new territories, and look deeply. We can well envision two-minute videos focused on one single ancestor, his life or her story, and how it illuminates our family's history and the bigger world. Or tell a single story. Or focus on a single place. The metaphor of the zoom lens applies here. The student can stand back and describe the great sweep of events, or pull in close to see how small things reflect the large.

Back to our example: At Upward Bound, the students were hurried into a room to shoot their videos on the last day of class, between this and that test, lunch, a trip to somewhere, and catching the bus home— seemingly not the best set of conditions. But one by one, they came in, each with a unique portfolio of materials and script. We elected (at the request of our video camera operator) to shoot documents laid out on tables in a brightly sunlit room. He held the camera perpendicular to the table and got right up close on every image: a Bible embossed as a gift from a trade union local containing birth records from the turn of the century, a seventy-year-old photograph of a deceased great-grandmother, a church brochure from Mexico showing a great-great-aunt, a nun who started her own religious order.

Here is Maggie Contreras's script:

My name is Margarita Contreras [*shot with picture of her next to map of Guanajuato, Mexico*]. I was born on March 24, 1981, in Uriangato, Guanajuato, Mexico. I'm going to tell of my paternal side of the family. My grandparents are Jose Contreras and Mary Margarita Zamudio [*shot with picture of her next to her kinship chart*]. Jose was born in Uriangato, Guanajuato. Mary Margarita Zamudio, who I was named after, was born in Evans, Colorado, in 1925 [*picture of fieldhands, wielding their hoes*]. I always heard that she used to wait anxiously every sunset for her father Francisco Zamudio to come home from the beet field.

[*shot of National Archives name from brochure cover*] During the project, I took a little trip with my class to the National Archives to view the census to find out if someone else from the family was in Colorado before my great-grandfather Francisco [*shot of the census pages with Zamudio family highlighted*]. To my surprise, I found in the 1920 census that Francisco came first in 1917 to work in the beet fields [*picture of the family, close up, showing mainly Francisco*]. After he settled in, one year later the rest of the family came to join him—my great-great-grandma, Valeria Torres; his wife, Leonor Billagomez;

and his daughter Jesus [*picture of the family, wider angle, showing the rest of the family*]. They all migrated for the need of money, to support the family, and to live a better life.

Antonio was the last person to come in on that last day. His family had only just immigrated from Mexico in 1993. All his family records, photos, and artifacts were still in his hometown of Durango. So all he had was a large map of Mexico, the family genealogical chart, and a recent photo of himself at school. With these three artifacts, Antonio wrote a script that described how, in the process of filling out his chart, he discovered that although he was born in Durango, no one else in his family was. Most of his family came from Zacatecas, where for generations they had farmed and ranched. They'd migrated to Durango in the 1950s.

The way this played out in the two-minute videotape shows how well script writing can work as a tool for pulling together the threads of a family story and how group work can enhance the construction of meaning and final product. A transparency was placed over the map of Durango and Zacatecas, and while Antonio read about this internal migration, a red marker was used to trace the path his family had taken. We searched through books and found photographs of land and of the cattle ranching the family was involved in. We came perilously close to shooting a photograph of Pancho Villa with a huge sombrero, mounted on a horse, and suggesting that it was Antonio's grandfather on his journey to Durango. We returned to a North American map and transparency to trace the migration from Durango to Chicago, and then searched in vain for a photo image of Chicago to end with. Finally, someone pointed to the huge windows that lined one wall. There stood the twin spires of the Sears tower and the cluster of skyscrapers rising out of the smog and factories. We had our shot. Antonio's script ended: "Doing this research makes me want to return to Durango and make the journey back to Zacatecas, the birthplace of my parents."

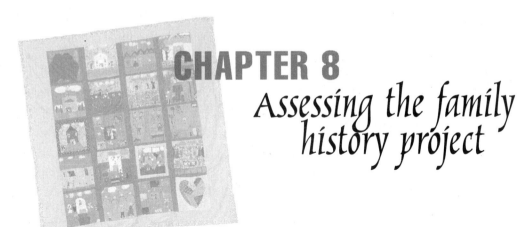

# CHAPTER 8
## Assessing the family history project

*t*eachers—and most adults in America—are thoroughly ambivalent about tests, grades, and assessment in general. Frequently when we talk with teachers about trying a new classroom activity such as the family history project, their first question is, "But how will I give this a grade?" Teachers fear that if a grade isn't easily assignable, somehow the project won't be worthwhile, they won't be able to justify it to their principal, and kids won't be motivated to do the work. On the other hand, if assessment eats up a lot of time, it will tie up the teacher's work schedule and prevent her from preparing for whatever follows the family history project. Parents often demand to know how their children rank in school, but recall feeling humiliated and discouraged when they themselves felt arbitrarily or unfairly evaluated by teachers in school.

Teachers have "accountability" worries. If a project doesn't center on specific, explicit skills and then test them, many teachers may ask, how will we know if the kids have learned anything? This question is driven by the standardized tests that eat up more and more time and energy with each successive school year. Teachers worry that if they spend lots of time on activities such as family history, they won't be able to "cover" all the skills for the upcoming tests. If the kids don't do well on the tests, the district will hold the teachers and principals accountable.

Ironically, the suburban schools that do well on the standardized tests usually devote more time to large projects with complex outcomes. Meanwhile, urban schools that serve lots of disadvantaged kids—kids who often see no connection between rote school exercises and their lives or their futures—are the schools where teachers are told to heap on still more disconnected, test-oriented drills. In fact, many of the standardized tests are designed to reward strong vocabulary, broad knowledge that comes from extensive reading, and practice at drawing inferences, all of which are strengthened by larger, more complex study activities, rather than by skill-and-drill exercises.

How, then, can assessment serve a more positive role in classroom inquiry activities such as family history? Good teachers often say they want assessment to:

1. reflect the teacher's own significant teaching goals;
2. support good instruction;
3. encourage students' growth and learning;
4. involve students in meaningful ways in the assessment process;
5. respond to parents and community needs for accountability in reasonable and meaningful ways;
6. use time and energy within reasonable limits.

We'll explore how assessment of students' work on family history can embody these principles. That way, when a teacher chooses to adopt a particular idea or suggestion, she'll have a clear sense of why it's being offered and what she can expect it to achieve.

## how-to guide
### STEPS 1 AND 2:
### CONSIDER HOW YOU WILL LINK ASSESSMENT OF FAMILY HISTORY TO YOUR TEACHING GOALS AND INSTRUCTIONAL ACTIVITIES

Before you begin to gather final products or decide how to grade students' work, it's important to consider what you hope to achieve. What do you hope the students will learn? What will the class be spending the most time on? Many teachers will turn to their district or state list of learning objectives in English and social studies to review their goals—and later we'll illustrate how teachers can reassure themselves that family history projects can address those objectives. But it's also important to remind yourself about your own most strongly held beliefs and principles that guide your teaching, for the official lists often omit knowledge and abilities we know are crucial to student development and success. These may include abilities to:

- ◆ work cooperatively and independently;
- ◆ choose intelligently among topics for writing and books to read;
- ◆ search persistently and resourcefully for new information;

◆ make connections between various subjects and between topics studied and real life experiences and challenges;

◆ ask probing and productive questions;

◆ draw thoughtful and creative conclusions from data.

Look, too, at how you use time in the classroom. If you and the children work hard on a particular set of concepts or learning strategies, let assessment reflect those, rather than focus on some extraneous items tacked onto the end of the project. Refer to your own list of goals and the work that you emphasize as you move through the following steps to decide on assessment strategies, and consider each strategy carefully to determine whether your own goals are being supported by what you do.

## STEP 3:
## USE ASSESSMENT STRATEGIES THAT ENCOURAGE STUDENTS' GROWTH

To help students grow, the teacher needs to find out how each one is doing and what help each one needs. Although she may collect finished work, the teacher can help more effectively if she intervenes early, while students are still engaged. To achieve this, she needs to observe each student's work informally, record the information, and respond immediately with one-on-one help or whole-class lessons, as needed.

Individual teacher-student conferences are key for this kind of assessment. Many teachers wish to use them but aren't sure how to keep the class productive while working with one student at a time. One essential is to make sure everyone is occupied while conferences occur. A chart listing steps in the activity, or options if a student is finished, with verbal reminders as needed, can help students stay on task.

A variety of management techniques keep the conferences going smoothly and efficiently. The teacher moves from desk to desk, rather than having students line up and fidget at the front of the room, so that they continue working while she conducts the conferences. On a list of the students, or a separate sheet for each student, she jots quick shorthand observations as she goes. And she asks questions before giving instruction so that she learns as much as possible about what students are thinking.

We described teacher-student conferences briefly in Chapter 4. Here are a few pointers for making them productive:

### Ask Questions

Rather than reading the student's work and offering an immediate suggestion, gather as much information as you can first, so you know where the student is in the process and what he or she is trying to achieve. Ask questions such as, "So what is this project about?" "What's the main thing you hope someone will learn from it?" "What part do you feel best about?" "What led you to focus on this topic?" "What stage are you at? What part are you working on now?"

### Have the Student State What Help She Needs

If students know that you expect them to state which aspect of the project they want help on, they'll take time for self-assessment before they request a conference. This creates a verbal contract in which the student has agreed in advance to work on improvements, so you don't get caught in a tug of war in which the student resists making changes you have urged.

### Teach Just One Skill or Strategy

Keep in mind that your aim is to help students learn how to improve their work, not just to achieve a perfect product. By focusing on one element, you allow the student to focus and remember the lesson, and avoid overwhelming her with more criticism than she is prepared to absorb. At the end of the conference, ask the student to state what he or she will do next. This cements the verbal contract and shows you where the student is headed.

### Use Shorthand Notes to Keep a Record

Bonnie Campbell Hill and Cynthia Ruptic, in *Practical Aspects of Authentic Assessment* (1994) suggest that teachers use Post-it notes to briefly record the outcome of conferences. The teacher transfers the notes at a later time to separate record sheets for each student, without having to recopy anything. This creates an in-depth anecdotal record of work with each student, at almost no additional time investment. The Post-its also allow the teacher to observe who is receiving attention from her, and who may have been neglected.

Student-teacher conferences focus assessment on growth as students are working, whereas folders and portfolios allow us to create a longitudinal record of that growth. Looking at students' improvement does *not* mean we are focusing on "effort" instead of "quality." Rather, it means that we ask what the student has *learned*, what aspects of the student's work are "value added," what new material has been contributed by ourselves as teachers, by the student as an active agent in his or her own growth, and by the project as a learning experience.

To achieve this perspective, we cannot assess family history products in isolation. Each student's portfolio needs a number of sheets or forms that document longer-range progress. These can include:

- a goal sheet—goals the student has set for the quarter or semester that have been negotiated with the teacher, with space for the student and the teacher to make periodic notations about progress toward these goals;
- lists of particular skills the student has learned—including writing skills, analytical skills, and subject-area skills such as map reading and time-line construction;
- vocabulary and spelling lists;
- lists or logs indicating books the student has read and the student's responses to them;
- rubrics that describe achievement on items completed over the course of the project;
- reflection pieces in which students write about what they've learned and how they've improved over time.

Since the family history project may be used at a variety of grade levels and may include a wide or narrow integration of school subjects, we won't identify specific content items or skills to be included in this longitudinal assessment process. Teachers will naturally plug in the concepts and skills they've stressed during the period of the project. But we do suggest that any rubrics focused on individual student products or performances be designed to stress growth, and that they be made flexible to include students' self-selected goals. Such a rubric might look like Figure 8.1.

## STEP 4:
## INVOLVE STUDENTS MEANINGFULLY IN THE ASSESSMENT PROCESS

When students assess themselves, they are able to speak from a particular perspective. They know from within which parts of the work were challenging and which were easy, which steps were new to them, which discoveries have stayed with them, and which promptly faded into the background. However, we need to cultivate the habit of self-assessment by asking students to engage in it regularly, allowing time for journal jottings at the end of a period or a project, and modeling so they can see how an adult goes about the task. Self-reflection is essential for making portfolios work. It turns bare artifacts into richly revealing histories of learning.

Here are the questions that Hebron Middle School teacher Jane

Choose a number for each "multiplier" to increase the score value of an area recently taught, and/or an area that individual student has chosen to improve. Multiply the raw score (of 1 to 5) by the "multiplier" to get the point total for each category. For example, for a student who worked hard on "elaboration," use multiplier of 10, compared with 5 for other items. This way, the total score will reflect the student's improvement, not just an arbitrary sum of points.

| Aspect of Project | Importance Multiplier | S | c | o | r | e | Point Totals |
|---|---|---|---|---|---|---|---|
| Quality of Ideas (includes important concepts, connects family and public history) | | 1 | 2 | 3 | 4 | 5 | |
| Elaboration (includes enough detail to help reader understand concepts) | | 1 | 2 | 3 | 4 | 5 | |
| Clear Expression of Ideas | | 1 | 2 | 3 | 4 | 5 | |
| Makes Presentation Interesting | | 1 | 2 | 3 | 4 | 5 | |
| Conventions (improved in areas listed in student's own goals) | | 1 | 2 | 3 | 4 | 5 | |
| Individual Goal Identified by Student | | 1 | 2 | 3 | 4 | 5 | |
| Individual Goal Identified by Student | | 1 | 2 | 3 | 4 | 5 | |
| Additional Unanticipated Achievement | | 1 | 2 | 3 | 4 | 5 | |

FIGURE 8.1

Sample flexible rubric for family history project

Sanders Boyce poses when she asks her students to reflect on their learning in the family history project:

- What did you learn about your family from interviewing family members?
- What are some things you never knew before?
- How did family members feel about helping you with this project?
- Do you have new feelings about your family members you didn't have before? (Some examples are pride in a certain person or in your heritage, or new respect for a certain family member.)

As with the previous step, portfolios are a key tool for making student involvement in assessment possible. Some pointers on organizing portfolios:

### Include a Wide Variety of Material in a Family History Portfolio

Of course, there are the specific products of the various family history activities, such as written portraits, completed questionnaires, kinship charts, time lines, pieces of art, and two-minute videos. If document copies are obtained from the National Archives or other sources, add them. Include family pictures, and any letters sent to and from more distant relatives. Other, more informal documents may well get created along the way—journal entries, sketches, the student's reflection pieces, and written comments on the student's work by peers and parents.

### Use Reflection to Engender Further Learning

Each major item in the portfolio should have a reflective comment attached that explains why it is important to the student and how it figured in the process of inquiry about his or her family. Although items can be assembled and reflections written at the end of the project, it's far better to add pieces gradually, have students look them over, and write reflections as they go. Help students think of the portfolio as a historical record that compares their perceptions, learning, and abilities at the beginning of the project with their achievements at the end. Pose reflective questions that ask students to take note of what they've learned thus far and to choose and write down one thing they'll work to improve in the coming weeks. Multiple drafts of written pieces help to show this progression, too. This way, the portfolio is part of an ongoing learning process. And you avoid expending a large amount of class time at the end of the project on the portfolio itself.

## Develop a Grading System for the Portfolio that Reflects What You and the Students Value

Some teachers "grade" the portfolio as a whole, whereas others give credit for the individual tasks, items, and activities that go into it. You may have a list of essential items that should be included in each portfolio, but be sure also to recognize items the student considers especially important. Give credit for the reflection pieces as well as the formal project items. Provide recognition for demonstrated learning and improvement. Include input on grades from the students themselves. Teachers find that separate from grades, most students take great pride in the assembled collection of their work, making art-filled covers, detailed tables of contents, and decorated section dividers to guide the reader.

Some helpful books on portfolio assessment are: Donald Graves and Bonnie Sunstein, eds., *Portfolio Portraits*; Carol Porter and Janell Cleland, *The Portfolio as a Learning Strategy*; Robert Tierney, Mark Carter, and Laura Desai, *Portfolio Assessment in the Reading-Writing Classroom*; and Kathleen Blake Yancey, ed., *Portfolios in the Writing Classroom*.

Student involvement in the process may involve not only self-assessment, but assessing peers. If we ask students to assess one another, however, the process gets more complicated. There is the danger that students may go easy on friends or hard on enemies. Parents may question the fairness of the grades. But assessment can accomplish much more important things than just giving grades, and we don't necessarily need to hand students that part of the task. Instead, we can ask students to share their work in small groups, recognizing that turning over ideas together often leads students to expressive possibilities they might not otherwise have tried. And when students write stories and reports, produce videos, and participate in panels, they need response from all sorts of audiences to see how their expression is received and interpreted. Such interchange is essential to learning the art of effective communication. Until we observe how our words are received by various audiences, we don't fully understand how those words work.

However, teachers don't necessarily get good results by simply turning students loose to give responses to one another in their small groups. The kids need guidance and training. One especially effective process is to hold small-group conferences in which the teacher talks over one student's work while several others listen in. That way, the students get to observe a competent adult as she provides supportive critiquing. If they see a good teacher ask lots of questions, rather than issue absolute instructions on how to improve, they'll quickly learn to do that themselves.

## STEP 5:
## RESPOND TO PARENT AND COMMUNITY NEEDS FOR ACCOUNTABILITY IN REASONABLE AND MEANINGFUL WAYS

The process of reporting to parents and the community through the impersonal and decontextualized modes of standardized tests and report cards can easily become burdensome and disconnected from learning. There are more meaningful ways of asking the larger community to respond to students' work, and we'll begin with those. One advantage of bringing other adults into the assessment process is that we gain fresh pairs of eyes, response from people who have not spent extensive periods of time watching the students' projects develop. They don't see all the work that may have gone into the projects, but they may notice features teachers have observed so often that they no longer appreciate them. Some schools—Central Park East Secondary School in New York for one—have highly formalized this process, requiring seniors to prepare presentations for invited panels of adults as a graduation requirement. We believe it's less important for parents or guests to "judge" family history projects than for them to give substantive feedback about their content. If you are conducting a family history fair, provide a pad next to each project for viewers to write responses. Next to the pad, the teacher or student can place a list of two or three questions to guide the viewers' responses, since most parents won't have prior experience with this kind of interaction. Then explicitly ask visitors to write comments. Assessment is implicit in this situation: students know their work will be viewed by a larger community, so they think about this larger audience as they learn, rather than only at the end of the process. The anticipation of bringing the community into the school and creating a real audience for kids' work completes the circle of the family history project, feeding back to the community the knowledge the students have gained. This lends an importance and a seriousness to the work that cannot be attained any other way.

When it comes to communicating to parents about individual students' progress, we're accustomed to sending home report cards with a single letter or number for each subject—not a very extensive or helpful picture of what the student has learned. Some schools and districts make their report cards more detailed, with lots of numbers or boxes to check off for a variety of subskills. But the majority of parents most appreciate seeing their children's work in depth, with information from the teacher on what it all means, including the student's growth, strengths, and areas that need work. A particularly effective way to achieve this is through *student-led parent conferences*, using the student's portfolio to display his or her work. The teacher joins in the conference and adds comments as needed. Teachers who use this strategy find that the students are more highly motivated to get their work done, and become more thoughtful and reflective as they describe what they've achieved. Class time and instructions must be provided so the students are thoroughly prepared to conduct the conference. This is time well spent, an additional exercise in good communication that challenges students to express themselves clearly. Some pointers on conducting student-led parent conferences:

### Prepare a Guide to Help Students Organize the Information They Will Give Parents or Guardians

Your guide can list key items about which you'd like students to reflect and comment. It might look like the example in Figure 8.2. When you allow time for students to go through this guide, write their answers, and get ready for the conference, you will add one more occasion for students to reflect on their work.

### Prepare a Short Explanation for Parents on What to Expect and How to Respond in the Student-Led Conference

Since most parents will not have experienced student-led conferences, it's a good idea to prepare them for the experience. In a letter, explain how the conference will work. To conserve time, three to four families may view their children's work simultaneously in separate corners of the room, according to a schedule you send out. You can circulate to each one to comment and answer any questions from parents. In your parent instruction letter, explain that it's the child's job to explain the work to the parents, and that this itself is an important educational experience. Suggest that parents pick two or three items in the student's portfolio to comment on. Emphasize that it's less important to praise or criticize than to ask questions, to tell the child what aspects of each item stand out, and to indicate what they, the parents, have learned from the portfolio.

### Plan Back-up Arrangements for Students Whose Parents or Guardians Do Not Attend the Conferences

To make sure every student has an adult audience for his or her conference, plan a period during school hours for those children whose

| Items and Questions | How I'll explain this to my parents |
|---|---|
| **Items in my portfolio—required** | |
| | |
| | |
| | |
| **Items in my portfolio—my own choices** | |
| | |
| | |
| | |
| **Skills I've learned this term, and which portfolio items show them** | |
| | |
| | |
| | |
| **Other ways I've improved** | |
| | |
| | |
| | |
| **Things I'm still trying to get better at** | |
| | |
| | |
| | |

FIGURE 8.2

Guide for students to prepare for student-led parent conferences parents do not attend on the conference night. Draft the principal, assistant principal, parent volunteers, and/or other adults in the building to come and review portfolios with the children. Be sure these adults are given the same instructions for responding that the parents receive.

At the most public and decontextualized level, informing a school board or other government agency about students' achievement presents some particular issues. Outside agencies want all students measured on the same scale, using the same testing procedures. They focus their concern on a set of skills or standards that supposedly reflect an adequate public education. However, the tests cannot take into account the special projects that teachers create to make learning meaningful and exciting, or the individual discoveries that hardworking, successful students make as they pursue these projects. Thus, although they supposedly measure everyone in the same way, standardized tests actually tell us very little about what students are learning. Also, they tend to discriminate against students who don't share the mainstream cultural background that most of the tests are designed to assume. Nevertheless, since this kind of assessment represents a political reality in American education today, we must find ways to cope with it and still carry out important teaching and learning activities.

Here is our solution. Many state tests are keyed to the state's lists of goals and objectives, so if the teacher compares, or "back-maps" from her project to the required state goals, she can determine which of these she has addressed in her project. Teachers often discover that in the course of an extensive inquiry project, they've served far more of the required goals than they first realized. Then, if some learning goals have not been covered, the teacher must plan to address them separately, before or after the project is completed. The assessment, in this case, is carried out by the state or the district, not the individual teacher. But the "back-mapping" reassures teacher, parents, and principal that the teaching expected by the community is being accomplished. We've provided an example of teachers back-mapping their middle school family history project in the Reality Checks just ahead.

## STEP 6:
## KEEP TIME AND ENERGY ON ASSESSMENT TO REASONABLE LIMITS

Many teachers feel obligated to assess student work continuously, because they fear that if they do not, students will not be motivated to carry it out. Yet this traditional purpose for assessment, based on principles of behavior modification, is extremely problematic and filled with contradictions. Educational experts such as Alfie Kohn (*Punished by Rewards: The Trouble with Gold Stars, Incentive Plans, A's, Praise, and Other Bribes*) point out that it never really works as intended. We've observed in classroom after classroom that when the work is intrinsically interesting and engaging, most students become involved and think very little about the grades they will get. Conversely, when students are unmotivated, holding out a grade usually does little to turn them around. When grades do have an effect, it's often not what we intended. In highly competitive social settings, teachers observe with frustration as kids worry about the grade but pay little attention to the ideas they are supposedly exploring. In other classrooms, the kids may work harder as quarterly grades come due, but then let work slide as the new quarter begins, the "reward" backfiring as much as it helps. Nevertheless, since most school systems do require grades, the best teachers can do is pursue more meaningful approaches, underplay the behavioral side as much as possible, and keep time and energy devoted to assessment to reasonable limits.

A good formula for controlling and focusing time spent on assessment is to:

- *frequently* gather your own descriptive information and give students supportive feedback—every day, or every time students work on family history projects in class;
- *periodically* pause for you and the students to reflect on progress and improvement—every week or two, as you move from one stage to the next in a project;
- *occasionally* give grades—when a whole project or unit is completed.

Some pointers for controlling time spent on assessment:

### To Monitor Small Steps in a Project, Check Off Items as You Circulate Around the Room

You do not need to collect and give letter grades for every detail of students' work. Student-teacher conferences will allow you to observe students' efforts and provide individualized help.

### Take Only a Portion of Student Folders or Portfolios Home to Review on a Given Night

Rotate your assessment process through the classroom, rather than overburdening yourself. If the stack is too high, you're more likely to rush through it, keep the folders too long while the students need them, or burn out and abandon the whole approach.

### Limit and Focus the Aspects of Students' Work That You Evaluate

Students (or anyone, for that matter) can process only so much feedback at one time. By focusing on one need or issue, you can help the student perceive patterns in his or her work. In contrast, if you mark or comment on every error in a problem-filled project, it will take lots of time that is unlikely to yield the improvement you seek. Remember that if your response has led to actual improvement, the assessment is supporting learning—even if you and the student have not yet addressed every skill on your list.

### Trade Off One Form of Assessment for Another

If you add student-teacher conferences to your repertoire, plan to subtract something else. They'll take time. You may find you are able to omit lectures and focused lessons on some topics, because students really do remember and apply what you've taught in your brief one-on-one helps. You'll have fewer problems to respond to when checking over completed drafts, because the student will have worked on them during classroom workshop time.

### Remind Yourself of Your Deepest Goals for the Family History Project

We hope that what you'll be seeking and finding as you go through this project is a more positive, respectful learning community in your classroom, students' increased self-respect and knowledge about their own heritage and its connection with others, and a fuller commitment to their learning because they see its connection with their own lives. You and the parents and the principal will be able to see when this is happening. And you won't need a letter grade to tell you that.

## reality checks
### A MIDDLE SCHOOL TEACHER PLANS HER CONTRACT-BASED ASSESSMENT SYSTEM

At Hebron Middle School in Hebron, Indiana, Jane Sanders Boyce knows the community expects grades for the students, but she wants them to serve as a record of work the students have completed and particular skills they have learned. Therefore, at the start of each week she posts a list of tasks that students must complete to receive a C, a B, or an A. As Jane Sanders Boyce explains,

> I tell them to decide what level they're aiming for this week. Then as I meet with individuals during the week, or conduct a "status of the class" check-in, I keep track of how each student is doing. Since these are middle school students, their moods swing up and down, so some students who aim for an A one week will aim lower the next. However, if a student is consistently not doing enough of the work, I make sure to have a conference with him or her, or talk to the parents.
>
> Each week I ask students to work on some specific tasks and skills, so rather than give grades on whether or not a piece of writing is perfect, I focus the grade on that week's particular tasks and skills. One week, I gave credit for completing at least six pages of interview notes. Another week, we worked on revision, and in particular on developing good leads and using logical paragraph divisions. If a student followed directions correctly in carrying out these tasks, he or she received the credit.
>
> I don't give a separate grade for the final book of essays and interviews each student puts together. Instead, I want to keep the emphasis on learning various writing and thinking skills each week. At the end of the project, however, students make up a grid that lists all the pieces they have put into their books. The essays may not be perfect, but it's gratifying to see how much pride students take in their work, and how many optional pieces the students include beyond those that are required.
>
> We should never underestimate what our students can teach us. Or how much they can entertain us.

## STUDENT REFLECTIONS ON THE FAMILY HISTORY AND DECADES PROJECT, SALINE MIDDLE SCHOOL

- I think it's amazing what you learn about family history. I learned that my 5th great-grandfather on my father's side, Ezekiel Smith, was one of 75 men on the green when the shot was fired at the start of the revolution and that he survived.
- I learned that my grandpa was going to play baseball in the minors but instead he got drafted into the Korean War.

- I think we need to do more about our families and this is a good way to do it.
- I am part Cherokee and kind of feel connected with the people on the Trail of Tears. I have discovered a lot of things I never knew before.
- I found out I am related to Gloria Swanson. . . . It's kind of neat being related to a movie star.
- I learned lots about my family. The only reason I didn't know much about them was because I was adopted when I was about eleven or so. . . . I feel real interested to hear about a family I didn't know anything about. It was very interesting.
- I got to find out things that I never knew before. . . . I am related to President John Tyler by marriage . . . that was really cool. I also found letters written during the Civil War by my great-grandfather.
- I learned my great-grandfather fought in the battle of the 19th Ohio Infantry in the Civil War.
- I thought the project was very informative and that it's good to learn about your past.
- I think that digging up your family history can be fun, but it is very time consuming and frustrating. . . . I felt that this project was exciting to find out who I was related to and where all my ancestors came from . . . that my great-grandpa's brother captured the world's largest Japanese flag during WWII.
- I have learned so much! I learned that there was a big stock market crash in 1929. I also learned that this really affected my very own family! My great-grandfather's business went bankrupt.
- I learned that I'm related to Abraham Lincoln and my friend is related to John Wilkes Booth.
- I learned in my research that the Sundance Kid, one of the most notorious bandits of all time, was my great uncle. He was my grandmother's brother. My great-great-grandfather was George Washington's personal protector.
- I learned that my mom's grandma lost her farm because of the Depression. . . . All of the prices dropped so much that they had to mortgage their farm.
- I discovered that I am related to former president William Henry Harrison.

## SALINE MIDDLE SCHOOL TEACHERS BACK-MAP TO MAKE SURE THEY'VE COVERED STATE AND DISTRICT GOALS

Following are goals and outcomes the teacher team determined were covered by the family history and decades project:

# Michigan State Outcomes:

*Language Arts*

- Content Standard 1. Students will read and comprehend general and technical material.
- Content Standard 2. All students will demonstrate the ability to write clear and grammatically correct sentences, paragraphs, and compositions.
- Content Standard 3. All students will focus on meaning and communications as they listen, speak, view, read, and write in personal, social, occupational, and civic contexts.
- Content Standard 4. All students will use the English language effectively.
- Content Standard 5. All students will read and analyze a wide variety of classic and contemporary literature and other texts to seek information, ideas, enjoyment, and understanding of their individuality, *our common heritage and common humanity, and the rich diversity in our society.*
- Content Standard 6. All students will learn to communicate information accurately and effectively and demonstrate their expressive abilities by creating oral, written, and visual texts that enlighten and engage an audience.

# Social Studies

*Core Democratic Values Stressed:*
   *Fundamental Beliefs:*
- Life
- Liberty
- The pursuit of happiness
- Diversity

*Constitutional Principles:*
- Individual rights
- Freedom of religion

## Saline Area Schools Language Arts Program Outcomes:

- Communicate effectively using reading, writing, speaking, and listening skills.
- Demonstrate the use of appropriate syntax, grammar, punctuation, spelling, and vocabulary.
- Gather, organize, and present information in a purposeful manner.
- Use a variety of resources and available technologies to access information, improve skills, and develop final products.
- Use problem-solving and teaming skills.
- Be an active, critical reader in various genres.
- Demonstrate an awareness of and respect for oneself, for individual differences, and for cultural diversity.

## Saline Area Schools Social Sciences Program Outcomes:

- Use narratives and graphic data to describe the settings of significant events that shaped the development of the United States as a nation.
- Engage in activities intended to advance student views on both national and international policy.
- Examine the historical and contemporary role an industry has played and continues to play in a community.
- Use historical biographies to explain how events from the past affected the lives of individuals and how some individuals influenced the course of history.
- Describe how social and scientific changes in regions may have global consequences.

## Saline Area Schools Science Program Outcomes:

- All students will have an understanding of science history and how it affects us today.
- All students will learn about scientists and their effect on history.
- All students will know and use all of the Multiple Intelligences.

### A TEACHER ASSESSES HER OWN WORK—REFLECTIONS ON THE VALUE OF TIME LINES

Teacher Karen Malhiot at Jenner School in Chicago has developed the idea of "time line in a box." Each student works with a long strip of butcher paper, folded accordion-style into about twenty sections, so that it will fit into a shoe box. The students start their time lines on a middle section and leave blank sections at the beginning and end—to add data about the past and the future as the year progresses. The "past" end of the strip is fastened to the bottom of the box, so the student can stretch out the strip to review it or add more dates and events. Karen reflects:

On New Year's Eve day, I sat down and created a time line of my life. New Year's is a time when I like to reflect on the past year, and after a very transitional year I felt the need to reflect on more of my life. Creating a time line gave me the chance to think about the many people who had been very influential in my life. For example, my Mormor (mother's mother) sold her successful business to get the money to move from Denmark to the United States, because she felt it was in the best interest of the family. She had always taught me to work hard and believe in myself. Additionally, it was a chance to reflect on the many events that have shaped me. One such event was a visit the past summer to Denmark with my mother. We traveled and saw many places and people who were influential in my mother's life. Having never been fascinated by history, I have found myself reflecting on the events that have shaped my grandparents' and my mother's past in Denmark, and how, ultimately, they have shaped my life. The process of examining these events and choosing those I wished to highlight in my time line has made me more aware of who I am, where I come from, and where I want to go.

I felt that this process, which has proved so rich for me, would make a wonderful process for my students to get a better sense of who they are. Now I struggle to discover how I can best facilitate this process of discovery in the classroom. I began by sharing my time line with the students and was startled by how interested they were in learning about my life—they are beginning to see me as a person and not just as a teacher. They were immediately interested in creating time lines of their own. We began to discuss the process of finding out about ourselves and how we could best discover the information we needed. Students left with questions they wanted to ask parents and family, and came back to class excited about sharing things they had discovered about themselves. One very shy student told a story about how her family thought she would be slow because she was so small when she was born, and now she is very smart. I find myself enjoying getting to know my students in a new way.

# state archives referral list

Alabama Department of Archives & History, 624 Washington Avenue, Montgomery, AL 36130

Alaska State Archives, 141 Willoughby Avenue, Pouch C, Juneau, AK 99811

Arizona State Library, Department of Library, Archives & Public Records, State Capitol, 1700 West Washington, Phoenix, AZ 85007

Arkansas History Commission, One Capitol Mall, Little Rock, AR 72201

California Office of the Secretary of State, California State Archives, 1020 O Street, Room 138, Sacramento, CA 95814

Colorado Department of Administration, Division of State Archives & Public Records, 1313 Sherman Street, 1-B20, Denver, CO 80203

Connecticut State Library, Archives, History & Genealogy Unit, 231 Capitol Avenue, Hartford, CT 06106

Delaware Division of Historical & Cultural Affairs, Bureau of Archives & Records Management, Hall of Records, Dover, DE 19901

Florida State Archives, R. A. Gray Building, 500 South Bronough Street, Tallahassee, FL 32399–0250

Georgia Department of Archives & History, 330 Capitol Avenue, SE, Atlanta, GA 30334

Hawaii Department of Accounting & General Services, Archive Division, Iolani Palace Grounds, Honolulu, HI 96813

Idaho State Historical Society, Division of Manuscripts & Idaho State Archives, 610 North Julia Davis Drive, Boise, ID 83702

Illinois Office of the Secretary of State, Archives Division, Archives Building, Springfield, IL 62756

Indiana State Library, Archives Division, 100 North Senate Avenue, Indianapolis, IN 46204

State Historical Society of Iowa, State Archives, Capitol Complex, Des Moines, IA 50319

Kansas State Historical Society, 120 West Tenth Street, Topeka, KS 66612

Kentucky Public Records Division, Archives Research Room, P.O. Box 537, Frankfort, KY 40602–0537

Louisiana Secretary of State, Archives & Records Division, P.O. Box 94125, Baton Rouge, LA 70804

Maine State Archives, State House-Station 84, Augusta, ME 04333

Maryland State Archives, 350 Rowe Boulevard, Annapolis, MD 21401

Massachusetts State Archives, Columbia Point, 220 Morrissey Boulevard, Boston, MA 02125

Michigan Department of State, Michigan History Division, State Archives Unit, 3405 North Logan Street, Lansing, MI 48906

Minnesota Historical Society, Division of Archives & Manuscripts, 1500 Mississippi Street, St. Paul, MN 55101

Mississippi Department of Archives & History, 100 South State Street, P.O. Box 571, Jackson, MS 39205

Director Records Management & Archives Service, Secretary of State's Office, P.O. Box 778, 1001 Industrial Drive, Jefferson City, MO 65102

Montana Historical Society, Division of Archives & Manuscripts, 225 North Roberts Street, Helena, MT 59601

Nebraska State Historical Society, State Archives Division, 1500 R Street, Lincoln, NE 68508

Nevada State Library & Archives, Division of Archives & Records, 101 South Fall Street, Carson City, NV 89710

New Hampshire Library & Archives, 71 South Fruit Street, Concord, NH 03301

New Jersey State Archives, Bureau of Archives & Records Preservation, CN-307, 185 West State Street, Trenton, NJ 08625

New Mexico State Records Center & Archives, Historical Services Division, 404 Montezuma, Santa Fe, NM 87503

New York State Archives, 11D40 Cultural Education Center, Albany, NY 12230

North Carolina State Archives, 109 East Jones Street, Raleigh, NC 27611

State Archives and Historical Research Library, North Dakota Heritage Center, Bismarck, ND 58505

The Ohio Historical Society, Archives-Manuscripts Division, 1985 Velma Avenue, Columbus, OH 43211

Oklahoma Department of Libraries, Archives & Records Division, 200 Northeast 18th Street, Oklahoma City, OK 73105

Oregon Secretary of State, Archives Division, Oregon State Archives & Records Center, 1005 Broadway NE, Salem, OR 97310

Pennsylvania State Archives, P.O. Box 1026, Harrisburg, PA 17108–1026

Rhode Island Secretary of State, Archives Division, Room 43, State House, Smith Street, Providence, RI 02903

South Carolina Department of Archives & History, P.O. Box 11669, Capitol Station, Columbia, SC 29211

South Dakota Department of Education & Cultural Affairs, South Dakota State

Archives, State Library Building, 800 Governors Drive, Pierre, SD 57501–2294

Tennessee State Library and Archives, 403 7th Avenue North, Nashville, TN 37219

Texas State Library, Archives Division, P.O. Box 12927, Austin, TX 78711

Utah State Archives & Records Service, State Capitol, Room B-4, Salt Lake City, UT 84114

Vermont Agency of Administration, Public Records Division, 6 Baldwin Street, Montpelier, VT 05602

Virginia State Library and Archives Division, 11th Street at Capitol Square, Richmond, VA 23219

Office of the Secretary of State, Division of Archives and Records Management, P.O. Box 9000, Olympia, WA 98504–9000

West Virginia Department of Culture and History, Archives and History Division, Science and Cultural Center, Capitol Complex, Charleston, WV 25305

State Historical Society of Wisconsin, Archives Division, 816 State Street, Madison, WI 53706

Wyoming Archives, Museum, and Historical Department, Archives and Records Management Division, Barrett Building, Cheyenne, WY 82002

# References

## Professional Books and Factual Information

Allerton, George. 1991. *Do It Yourself Family History: Our Family History and Records.* Orfield, PA: Associated Specialties Co.

Atwell, Nancie. 1998. *In the Middle: New Understandings About Writing, Reading and Learning,* 2d ed. Portsmouth, NH: Heinemann.

Beatty, Alexandra S., et al. 1996. *NAEP 1994 U.S. History Report Card.* Princeton, NJ: Educational Testing Service.

Blachowicz, Camille, and Peter Fisher. 1995. *Teaching Vocabulary in All Classrooms.* Englewood Cliffs, NJ: Prentice-Hall.

Calkins, Lucy. 1994. *The Art of Teaching Writing.* Portsmouth, NH: Heinemann.

Cunningham, Patricia. 1995. *Phonics They Use.* New York: HarperCollins.

Daniels, Harvey, and Marilyn Bizar. 1998. *Methods that Matter: Six Structures for Best Practice Classrooms.* York, ME: Stenhouse.

Divorce Centers, Inc. *Parents Handbook.*

Graves, Donald. 1994. *A Fresh Look at Writing.* Portsmouth, NH: Heinemann.

Graves, Donald, and Bonnie Sunstein, eds. 1992. *Portfolio Portraits.* Portsmouth, NH: Heinemann.

Hill, Bonnie Campbell, and Cynthia Ruptic. 1994. *Practical Aspects of Authentic Assessment.* Norwood, MA: Christopher Gordon.

Kohn, Alfie. 1993. *Punished by Rewards: The Trouble with Gold Stars, Incentive Plans, A's, Praise, and Other Bribes.* Boston: Houghton Mifflin.

Porter, Carol, and Janell Cleland. 1995. *The Portfolio as a Learning Strategy.* Portsmouth, NH: Heinemann.

Provenzo, Eugene, Jr., Asterie Baker Provenzo, and Peter A. Zorn, Jr. 1984. *Pursuing the Past: Teacher's Guide.* Reading, MA: Addison-Wesley.

Rogovin, Paula. 1998. *Classroom Interviews: A World of Learning.* Portsmouth, NH: Heinemann.

Short, Kathy G., et al. 1996. *Learning Together Through Inquiry: From Columbus to Integrated Curriculum*. York, ME: Stenhouse.

Short, Kathy G., Jerome C. Harste, and Carolyn Burke. 1996. *Creating Classrooms for Authors and Inquirers*. Portsmouth, NH: Heinemann.

Tierney, Robert, Mark Carter, and Laura Desai. 1991. *Portfolio Assessment in the Reading-Writing Classroom*. Norwood, MA: Christopher Gordon.

U.S. Bureau of Labor Statistics. 1997. *Employment Characteristics of Families, 1997*. Washington DC: U.S. Bureau of Labor Statistics.

U.S. Bureau of the Census. March 1998. *Household and Family Characteristics* (Current Population Reports #P20–515). Washington, DC: U.S. Bureau of the Census.

U.S. Bureau of the Census. March 1998. *Marital Status and Living Arrangements* (Current Population Reports #P20–514). Washington, DC: U.S. Bureau of the Census.

Wallis, Frank. 1988. *Ribbons of Time: World History Year by Year Since 1492*. New York: Weidenfeld and Nicolson.

Whitin, Phyllis. 1996. *Sketching Stories, Stretching Minds*. Portsmouth, NH: Heinemann.

Wilhelm, Jeffrey. 1997. *You Gotta BE the Book*. New York: Teachers College Press.

Yancey, Kathleen Blake, ed. 1992. *Portfolios in the Writing Classroom*. Urbana, IL: National Council of Teachers of English.

Zemelman, Steven, and Harvey Daniels. 1988. *A Community of Writers: Teaching Composition in the Junior and Senior High School*. Portsmouth, NH: Heinemann.

## Recommended Literature

Frank, Anne. 1993 edition. *Anne Frank: the Diary of a Young Girl*. New York: Bantam Books.

Frasier, Debra. 1995. *On the Day You Were Born*. New York: Harcourt Brace.

Garza, Carmen Lomas. 1990. *Family Pictures—Cuadros de Familia*. Emeryville, CA: Children's Book Press.

Hemingway, Ernest. 1995 edition. *For Whom the Bell Tolls*. New York: Scribner.

Houston, Jeanne Wakatsuki. 1983 edition. *Farewell to Manzanar*. New York: Bantam Starfire.

Hurston, Zora Neale. 1996 edition. *Dust Tracks on a Road*. New York: HarperCollins.

Kahn, Kathy. 1973. *Hillbilly Women*. New York: Avon Books.

Knight, Margy Burns. 1993. *Who Belongs Here? An American Story*. Gardiner, ME: Tilbury House.

Lawrence, Jacob. 1993. *The Great Migration*. New York: Museum of Modern Art.

Martin, Bill, and John Archambault. 1996. *Knots on a Counting Rope*. New York: Henry Holt.

Myers, Walter Dean. 1991 edition. *Fallen Angels*. New York: Scholastic Paperbacks.

Polacco, Patricia. 1988. *The Keeping Quilt*. New York: Simon & Schuster.

Santiago, Esmerelda. 1994. *When I Was Puerto Rican*. New York: Vintage.

Say, Allen. 1993. *Grandfather's Journey*. Boston: Houghton Mifflin.

## also of interest...

# The Parent Project
*A Workshop Approach to Parent Involvement*

**James Vopat**

**1994 • 248 pp/paper • 0001**

Parental involvement strengthens the link between home and school. To achieve this goal parents need to be introduced to the revitalized classroom. Using a workshop/process model, parents become involved with their children's classroom activities and support their children's education. The workshops ensure participant ownership of a program's overall agenda while providing long-term structures for support and continued development.

Developed in urban bilingual school settings, *The Parent Project*

◆ provides a framework for implementing ways to get parents involved and informed;

◆ is the first book to connect parents with progressive education and changes in today's classrooms;

◆ is a complete source-book for teachers and principals that provides materials for conducting workshops with parents in writing, reading, self-esteem, and community-building;

◆ provides a detailed description of what the workshop approach is and how it functions.

Includes reproducible workshop handouts and formats in Spanish and English.

# Methods that Matter
*Six Structures for Best Practice Classrooms*

## Harvey Daniels and Marilyn Bizar

**1998 • 272pp/paper • full-color insert • 0082**

Here are practical and proven ways of organizing time, space, materials, students, and activities that embody new standards while creating genuinely student-center classrooms. Illustrated by stories from two dozen teachers at a wide variety of grade levels, the book clearly describes six fundamental, recurrent activities in "Best Practice" classrooms:

- ◆ Integrative units—extending thematic, interdisciplinary inquiries co-planned with students, drawing on knowledge and skills from across the curriculum.
- ◆ Small group activities—structuring collaborative pairs, groups, and teams that decentralize the classroom and individualize the curriculum.
- ◆ Representing-to-learn—engaging ideas through writing and art; exploring genres and media of expression as ways of investigating, remembering, and applying information.
- ◆ Classroom workshop—applying the studio-apprenticeship method with teacher modeling and coaching, student choice, responsibility, and exhibition.
- ◆ Authentic experiences—curriculum-centered ways of bringing life into school and students into the community for research and service.
- ◆ Reflective assessment—nurturing student reflection, goal-setting, and self-assessment; widening the evaluative roles and repertoires of teachers and parents.

*Also available:* Study Guide for *Methods that Matter*
Includes suggestions for organizing a study group, chapter summaries, group and individual activities. Download a free copy from www.stenhouse.com.

**Printed Study Guide • 01ST**

Order from your authorized Stenhouse distributor
or call (800) 988-9812